Other books in the Travel Guide series include:

A Travel ✦ Guide to
THE HARLEM
JAZZ ERA

By Stuart A. Kallen

LUCENT BOOKS

THOMSON
———— ✦ ————
GALE

San Diego • Detroit • New York • San Francisco • Cleveland • New Haven, Conn. • Waterville, Maine • London • Munich

THOMSON
————★————™
GALE

LIBRARY OF CONGRESS CATALOGING-IN-PUBLICATION DATA

Kallen, Stuart A., 1955–
  The Harlem Jazz Era / by Stuart A. Kallen.
    p. cm. — (A travel guide to:)
Summary: A visitor's guide to the restaurants, theater, arts, dancing, and jazz music of Harlem, New York, toward the end of the period known as the Harlem Renaissance, when African American arts flourished.
Includes bibliographical references and index.
  ISBN 1-59018-358-4 (alk. paper)
1. African Americans—Intellectual life—20th century—Juvenile literature. 2. Harlem Renaissance—Juvenile literature. 3. Harlem (New York, N.Y.)—Intellectual life—20th century—Juvenile literature. 4. African Americans—New York (State)—New York—Intellectual life—20th century—Juvenile literature. 5. African American arts—New York (State)—New York—History—20th century—Juvenile literature. 6. Harlem (New York, (N.Y.)—Social life and customs—20th century—Juvenile literature. 7. New York, (N.Y.)—Intellectual life—20th century—Juvenile literature. 8. (New York, N.Y.)—Social life and customs—20th century—Juvenile literature. 9. Harlem (New York, N.Y.)—Guidebooks—Juvenile literature. [1. Harlem Renaissance. 2. African American arts. 3. African Americans—History—1877–1964. 4. Harlem (New York, N.Y.)—History.] I. Title. II. Travel Guide (Lucent Books).
  E185.6.K255 2004
  974.7'1—dc22
                                                                           2003014089

Printed in the United States of America

Contents

Foreword

Travel can be a unique way to learn about oneself and other cultures. The esteemed American writer and historian, John Hope Franklin, poetically expressed his conviction in the value of travel by urging, "We must go beyond textbooks, go out into the bypaths and untrodden depths of the wilderness and travel and explore and tell the world the glories of our journey." The message communicated by this eloquent entreaty is clear: The value of travel is to temper one's imagination about a place and its people with reality, and instead of thinking how things may be, to be able to experience them as they really are.

Franklin's voice is not alone in his summons for students to "travel and explore." He is joined by a stentorian chorus of thinkers that includes former president John F. Kennedy, who established the Peace Corps to facilitate cross-cultural understandings between Americans and citizens of other lands. Ideas about the benefits of travel do not spring only from contemporary times. The ancient Greek historian Herodotus journeyed to foreign lands for the purpose of immersing himself in unfamiliar cultural traditions. In this way, he believed, he might gain a first-hand understanding of people and ways of life in other places.

The joys, insights, and satisfaction that travelers derive from their journeys are not limited to cultural understanding. Travel has the added value of enhancing the traveler's inner self by expanding his or her range of experiences. Writer Paul Tournier concurs that, "The real meaning of travel, like that of a conversation by the fireside, is the discovery of oneself through contact with other people."

The Lucent Books Travel Guide series enlivens history by introducing a new and innovative style and format. Each volume in the series presents the history of a preeminent historical travel destination written in the casual style and format of a travel guide. Whether providing a tour of fifth-century B.C. Athens, Renaissance Florence, or Shakespeare's London, each book describes a city or area at its cultural peak and orients readers to only those places and activities that are known to have existed at that time.

A high level of authenticity is achieved in the Travel Guide series. Each book is written in the present tense and addresses the reader as a prospective foreign traveler. The sense of authenticity is further achieved, whenever possible, by the inclusion of descriptive quotations by contemporary writers who knew the place; information on fascinating historical sites; and travel tips meant to explain unusual cultural idiosyncrasies that give depth and texture to all great cultural centers. Even shopping details, such as where to buy an ermine-trimmed gown, or a much-needed house slave, are included to inform readers of what items were sought after throughout history.

Looked at collectively, this series presents an appealing presentation of many of the cultural and social highlights of Western civilization. The collection also provides a framework for discussion about the larger historical currents that dominated not only each travel destination but countries and entire continents as well. Each book is customized by the author to bring to the fore the most important and most interesting characteristics that define each title. High standards of scholarship are assured in the series by the generous peppering of relevant quotes and extensive bibliographies. These tools provide readers a scholastic standard for their own research as well as a guide to direct them to other books, periodicals, and websites that will provide them greater breadth and detail.

A New Day in Harlem

Harlem occupies less than three square miles of Manhattan Island in northern New York City and is home to more than 350,000 African Americans. In the past ten years, between 1919 and 1929, this crowded neighborhood has experienced an unprecedented revival based on African American art, literature, music, dance, and more. Called the "New Negro Renaissance" by some and the "Harlem Renaissance" by others, this whirlwind of creativity is unmatched anywhere else in the United States. And not only has the Harlem Renaissance transformed African American society, it has also influenced American culture in general. Never before have so many white Americans embraced the books, music, artwork, expressions, and fashion sense of African Americans.

The renaissance is being led by what author Alain Locke calls "the new Negro"[1] and today's Harlem has become a magnet for black dancers, singers, painters, playwrights, actors, and musicians, as well as businesspeople and tourists from across the globe. As author and educator James Weldon Johnson wrote in 1925: "Harlem is indeed the great Mecca for the sight-seer; the pleasure-seeker, the curious, the adventurous, the enterprising, the ambitious and the talented of the whole Negro world; for the lure of it has reached down to every island of the [Caribbean] Sea and has penetrated even into Africa."[2]

The Jazz Age

This renaissance is taking place at a time unlike any other in American history, what we today call the Roaring Twenties, the Flapper Era, or the Jazz Age. The word "jazz," a black slang term, is used by nearly everyone today. Fashionable clothes are "jazz dresses," modern syncopated verse is called "jazz poetry," and fast old cars are called "jazzy jalopies." The swinging jazz music can be heard floating out of bars, barbershops, and beauty parlors, and is played by live bands at dance halls, cabarets, and clubs.

This is happening as the American economy is growing at its fastest rate in history. The stock market today is soaring as a new class of millionaires, white and black, have been minted virtually overnight. Rich and poor alike are using their money to buy that great new invention, the radio, as well as new and improved phonographs that are making jazz music—some of it straight out of Harlem—available to millions of people for the first time.

It has become fashionable among whites to support many aspects of African American culture, including art, literature, music, and more. Plays, revues, and theatrical productions with all-black casts are packing in white audiences—an unprecedented meeting of the races with jazz music at its center.

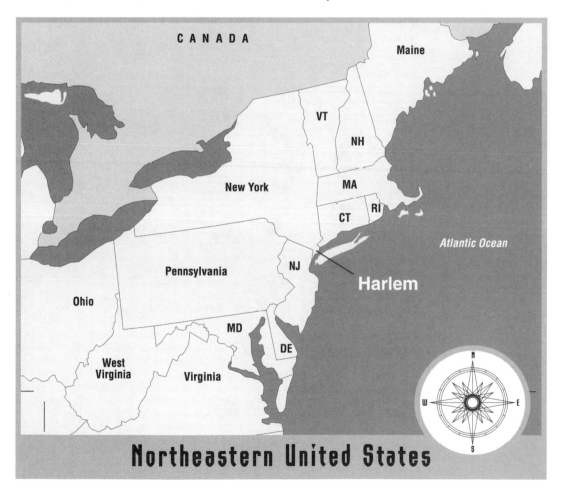

Northeastern United States

The Harlem Jazz Era

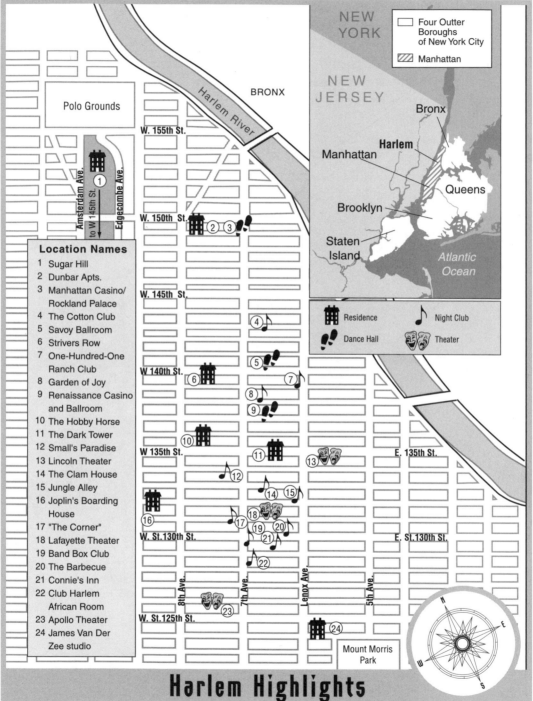

Harlem Highlights

Location Names
1 Sugar Hill
2 Dunbar Apts.
3 Manhattan Casino/ Rockland Palace
4 The Cotton Club
5 Savoy Ballroom
6 Strivers Row
7 One-Hundred-One Ranch Club
8 Garden of Joy
9 Renaissance Casino and Ballroom
10 The Hobby Horse
11 The Dark Tower
12 Small's Paradise
13 Lincoln Theater
14 The Clam House
15 Jungle Alley
16 Joplin's Boarding House
17 "The Corner"
18 Lafayette Theater
19 Band Box Club
20 The Barbecue
21 Connie's Inn
22 Club Harlem African Room
23 Apollo Theater
24 James Van Der Zee studio

Residence   Night Club   Dance Hall   Theater

Four Outter Boroughs of New York City   Manhattan

Source for map of Harlem: Steven Watson, *The Harlem Renaissance: Hub of African-American Culture, 1920–1930.* New York: Pantheon Books, 1995.

A Tourist Mecca

This revolution in economics, race relations, and culture has improved Harlem immeasurably. The people who make up the social fabric of Harlem—"the city within a city"—live in a neighborhood with beautiful buildings, well-lit streets, and bustling commercial districts. From the "Home of the Happy Feet" at the Savoy Ballroom on Lenox Avenue to the splendid restaurants on Sugar Hill, tourists will find no shortage of entertainment in the area. Those with the money to live in high style can rub elbows with the hottest new jazz acts at the Garden of Joy. Those with fewer dollars in their pockets can simply attend a rent party where fifty cents will gain one admission to a private party that will probably last until dawn.

Travelers, black or white, who want to experience the exciting and dynamic scene that is the Harlem Renaissance will be sure to find this volume useful. Some of you might be writers, painters, poets, or musicians traveling to Harlem to join in the renaissance. Others might be thinking of moving to the neighborhood to join fellow immigrants from Louisiana, Alabama, Mississippi, Georgia, the West Indies, or Africa. It matters little whether you are simply a tourist hoping to see history being made or hoping to make history yourself. This book will assist those who need to know the best places to stay, eat, shop, and find entertainment. Whatever your background and reason for travel, you are bound to have a grand time in Harlem, the jazziest neighborhood of the Jazz Age.

Chapter 1

The World's Greatest Negro Metropolis

The Harlem Renaissance began in earnest in 1919 after the end of World War I, when tens of thousands of black veterans returned to the neighborhood after serving valiantly on the battlefields of Europe. In the ten years since that time, Harlem has undergone a celebrated transformation. For tourists visiting the area, the fascinating history of this neighborhood can provide an interesting background to the exciting sights, sounds, and tastes of Harlem.

The district once known as Haarlem was originally settled by Dutch pioneers in the seventeenth century. In the following centuries the neighborhood became a magnet for German, Irish, and Jewish immigrants. While black people have always lived in New York City, most

The Old Stadt Huys of New Amsterdam.

resided on the southern part of Manhattan near Greenwich Village.

A History of Black Tenancy

The first influx of black residents to Harlem can be traced to a single apartment house at 31 West 133rd Street. This building was filled with black tenants in 1905 who were charged an extra five dollars more per month than whites (a common, if unfortunate, practice). Around this time a black real estate agent, Philip A. Payton Jr., organized the Afro-American Realty Company and began buying and leasing houses and apartments in Harlem specifically for occupancy by black people. White people in Harlem, however, were unhappy with this new development and formed organizations that loudly protested to banks that lent money to black people for real estate. The banks stopped lending, but despite this fact blacks were able to continue to move into Harlem while thousands of white people left. Johnson describes the circumstances:

> The situation . . . resolved itself into an actual contest. Negroes not only continued to occupy available apartment houses, but began to purchase private dwellings between Lenox and Seventh Avenues. Then the whole movement, in the eyes of the whites, took on the aspect of an "invasion"; they became panic-stricken and began fleeing as from a plague. The presence of one colored family in a block, no matter how well bred and orderly, was sufficient to precipitate a flight. House after house and block after block was actually deserted. It was a great demonstration of human beings running amuck. None of them stopped to reason why they were doing it or what would happen if they didn't. The banks and lending companies holding mortgages on these deserted houses were compelled to take them over. For some time they held these houses vacant, preferring to do that and carry the charges than to rent or to sell them

As black people moved into Harlem, white residents left the neighborhood, loudly criticizing banks for giving mortgages to the "invaders."

to colored people. But values dropped and continued to drop until, at the outbreak of war in Europe [in 1914], property in north Harlem had reached the nadir [lowest point].[3]

For once, racism benefited the black community. To compound the good news, there was a labor shortage in New York just as wartime industries were under orders to produce record numbers of armaments, clothes, rations, and other goods to fight World War I. For the first time, black laborers were making good wages that allowed them to save money. Meanwhile community leaders encouraged neighborhood residents to buy houses and apartments. For example, when the Metropolitan Baptist Church bought the beautiful brownstone church building on Seventh Avenue, Reverend

Black people found their labor in high demand as American industries struggled to meet the urgent need for weapons and supplies during World War I.

W.W. Brown, in his weekly sermons, urged his congregation to buy property. Many took his advice.

Home buying reached a fever pitch in 1920–1921, a time when common laborers had enough money saved to enable them to walk into real estate offices and lay down anywhere from one thousand dollars to five thousand dollars cash to purchase property. A legendary story in Harlem concerns "Pig Foot Mary" who to this day sells "soul food" such as fried chicken, pickled pigs' feet, and corn from a small stand on 135th and Lenox.

Mary was able to make enough from this enterprise to lay down forty-two thousand dollars cash for a five-story apartment house on Seventh Avenue and 137th Street. She made thirty thousand dollars on the property selling it to the YMCA several years later. Dozens of success stories of this type abound in the neighborhood and, in fact, the total value of property owned by blacks in Harlem today is an amazing $60 million. This number was achieved by people who were able to buy property at rock-bottom prices from banks, and resell it as prices skyrocketed. This buying and selling in Harlem has created some of the first black real estate moguls in New York history. As Johnson wrote in 1925:

[This] is amazing, especially when we take into account the short time in which [it happened]. Twenty years ago Negroes were begging for the privilege of renting a flat in Harlem. Fifteen years ago barely a half dozen colored men owned real property in all Manhattan. And down to ten years ago the amount that had been acquired in Harlem was comparatively negligible. Today Negro Harlem is practically owned by Negroes.[4]

Opportunity and Freedom

In this manner Harlem has been remade as the cultural capital of black America. As had happened in earlier centuries, the people new to Harlem have come from many parts of the globe, including Jamaica, Haiti, Cuba, Puerto Rico, Africa, and elsewhere. They are joining rural blacks migrating from the American South who have come to Harlem to escape widespread poverty

and the racial violence of the powerful Ku Klux Klan. But these migrants and immigrants did not move to Harlem simply to escape the negative but also to grab hold of positive opportunities and democratic change. As Alain Locke writes in his groundbreaking book, *The New Negro: An Interpretation:*

In the very process of being transplanted, the Negro is becoming transformed. . . . The tide of Negro migration, northward and cityward, is not to be fully explained as a blind flood started by the demands of war industry coupled with . . . the pressure of poor crops coupled with increased social terrorism in certain sections of the South and Southwest. Neither labor demand . . . nor the Ku Klux Klan is a basic factor. . . . The wash and rush

Blacks from around the globe poured into Harlem in the 1920s. Those from the American South came to escape the bigotry and brutality of the Ku Klux Klan (pictured).

of this human tide on the beach line of the northern city centers is to be explained primarily in terms of a new vision of opportunity, of social and economic freedom, of a spirit to seize, even in the face of an [expensive] and heavy toll, a chance for the improvement of conditions. With each successive wave of it, the movement of the Negro become

Who Lives in Harlem?

In the past twenty years, Harlem has become a melting pot for black cultures from across the globe. Visitors may wonder from where the new residents originate and their reasons for moving to Harlem. Those questions are answered by Alain Locke in *The New Negro: An Interpretation:*

Here in Manhattan is not merely the largest Negro community in the world, but the first concentration in history of so many diverse elements of Negro life. It has attracted the African, the West Indian, the Negro American; has brought together the Negro of the North and the Negro of the South; the man from the city and the man from the town and village; the peasant, the student, the business man, the professional man, artist, poet, musician, adventurer and worker, preacher and criminal, exploiter and social outcast. Each group has come with its own separate motives and for its own special ends, but their greatest experience has been the finding of one another. [Exclusion] and prejudice have thrown these dissimilar elements into a common area of contact and interaction. Within this area, race sympathy and unity have determined a further fusing of sentiment and experience. So what began in terms of segregation be-

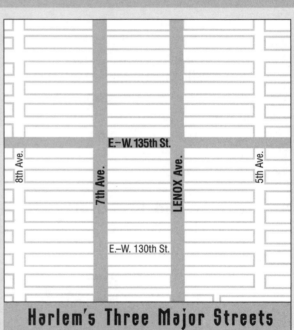

E.–W. 135th St.

8th Ave. 7th Ave. LENOX Ave. 5th Ave.

E.–W. 130th St.

Harlem's Three Major Streets

comes more and more, as its elements mix and react, the laboratory of a great race-welding. . . . In Harlem, Negro life is seizing upon its first chances for group expression and self-determination. It is—or promises at least to be— a race capital. . . . Without pretense to their political significance, Harlem has the same role to play for the New Negro as Dublin has had for the New Ireland or Prague for the New Czechoslovakia.

Despite their varied origins, blacks moving into Harlem have forged a strong sense of community.

more a mass movement toward the larger and the more democratic chance—in the Negro's case a deliberate flight not only from countryside to city, but from medieval America to modern.[5]

Mixed together in New York City, the quintessential American melting pot, this lively blend of cultures, languages, and religions has added a spice to Harlem society that can be found no-

where else. With such a background it is little wonder that the neighborhood has earned the name, "The World's Greatest Negro Metropolis."

As the black population stabilizes in Harlem, civic organizations have been formed and a tight-knit community has evolved. Today, tourists to the neighborhood that are members of the Elks, Freemasons, and other fraternal organizations will find lodges to visit in Harlem. Religious travelers will find dozens of churches, large and small, that cater to the black population.

Marching Home from War

By the late 1910s Harlem had become a mecca for black New Yorkers. But residents will tell you that the New Negro Renaissance was really launched on February 17, 1919. On that spectacular morning, thirteen hundred World War I veterans of the all-black 369th Infantry Regiment marched up Fifth Avenue. The infantry, known as the "Harlem Hellfighters," was composed of men who were the first black troops sent to fight on the European battlefront. Their acts of bravery in battle were legendary on both sides of the Atlantic.

The soldiers were politely cheered on by white citizens, including Governor Al Smith, as they marched down Fifth Avenue. But after crossing over to Lenox and passing 130th Street, the soldiers entered Harlem where they received a hero's welcome. As the *New York Age* newspaper wrote, the "Hellfighters marched between two howling walls of humanity."[6]

Leading the march were the sixty members of the Hellfighter's military band, led by James Reese Europe. As the band broke into a jazzy version of "Here Comes My Daddy," girlfriends and relatives joined the ranks of soldiers. Tenants on rooftops tossed a torrent of pennants, flags, banners, and scarves on the heroes.

When that band turned the corner onto Lenox and entered Harlem, the black community turned another corner. The new heroes of Harlem had returned home with a new style of music, a new dignity, and a new lifestyle. With so many willing to take risks to prove their worth to a society that never before valued their contributions, the New Negro Movement had begun. And Harlem would never be the same.

Marcus Garvey

After fighting in World War I, and being celebrated in Europe, and decorated in France, Harlem's black veterans were not content to quietly accept the prejudice so prevalent in America today. In order to combat the twin challenges of racism and urban poverty, African Americans in Harlem formed a host of political organizations to agitate for the rights of the black community.

Tips for Travelers

Veterans of the Harlem Hellfighters still meet at the 369th Regiment Armory on Fifth Avenue and 143rd Street. Tourists lucky enough to visit when Henry Johnson is there can meet the legendary man who fought off an entire German patrol single-handedly, killing four of the enemy and wounding several others though wounded himself. On display at the armory is the Croix de Guerre (Cross of War), the esteemed medal awarded by France to the entire regiment for their bravery.

On February 17, 1919, thirteen hundred World War I veterans of the all-black 369th Infantry Regiment parade triumphantly down Fifth Avenue and on to a thunderous reception in Harlem.

Visitors to Harlem interested in learning about the racial politics in America today can attend meetings at the Universal Negro Improvement Association (UNIA), located at 56 West 135th Street. For more than ten years, the UNIA has advanced the "Back to Africa" movement, calling for black people to return to Africa and start their own free nation.

The UNIA was founded in Harlem in 1916 by the charismatic leader Marcus Garvey, one of the leading forces for social and political change in Harlem in the past decade. Garvey also started the Black Star Line in 1919 to provide steamship transportation for manufactured goods, raw materials, and produce between black businesses in North America, the Caribbean, and Africa. Garvey's shipping line also attempted to attract Harlem tourist business. Unfortunately his luck with ships was poor. The SS *Shadyside* carried black passengers on excursions along the Hudson River, but sprang a leak and sank within a few months. The steam yacht SS *Antonio Maceo* awed visitors to the 135th Street dock in Harlem but blew a boiler and killed a man on its maiden voyage.

Despite these setbacks, by the early 1920s the UNIA claimed 2 million members worldwide. Money raised by Garvey was used to finance small businesses and factories for black employment in Harlem and elsewhere.

When Garvey's political views gained attention from the federal government, an investigation uncovered questionable business practices that resulted in the leader's imprisonment in 1925. In 1927 he was deported to his native Jamaica. Although the movement has foundered somewhat since Garvey's departure, the newspaper of the UNIA, the *Negro World*, is still published in Harlem. The UNIA also continues with other activities.

Female visitors to Harlem might be interested to know that the UNIA has long offered women important roles in the organization and has given them a chance to develop leadership and organizational skills. The Black Cross Nurses auxiliary, with chapters throughout the United States, Central America, and the Caribbean, is modeled on the Red Cross. It performs community work and public health services in black neighborhoods, specializing in infant health and home care. These nurses can be seen in long white robes or green nursing uniforms at

Travelers are welcome at meetings of the Universal Negro Improvement Association (UNLA), founded by political and social activist Marcus Garvey (pictured).

many of the dozens of parades held every year in Harlem.

Mechanically inclined women might seek out UNIA's Universal African Motor Corps, a female auxiliary trained in military discipline and automobile driving and repair.

Garvey also promoted a youth corps movement called the Juvenile Divisions. Children ages one through seven study the Bible and the history of Africa. Older girls are taught sewing, boys are taught woodcraft, and both receive further instruction in black history and etiquette. After the age of thirteen, boys receive military training while girls learn about hygiene and domestic arts in order to become members of the Black Cross Nurses. At parades boys in the Juvenile Divisions may be seen marching in blue uniforms with the girls in green dresses.

Black Leaders in Harlem Today

The UNIA is but one of the many black organizations in Harlem today that include the National Urban League, the National Association for the Advancement of Colored People (NAACP), and the socialist African Blood Brotherhood. Information regarding activities of these organizations may be found in their self-published newspapers available for fifteen cents throughout the neighborhood; the *Crisis* is published by the NAACP and *Opportunity* by the Urban League.

Africa

These papers, and others throughout Harlem, feature articles, essays, art, stories, and poems written by some of the leading voices of the New Negro Movement. W.E.B. Du Bois, founder of the NAACP, has written books that express the rage, sadness, and frustration of black Americans while encouraging blacks to become involved in government. His influence on black politics and social life is undisputed in Harlem.

"Nothing Just Like It"

The story of black Harlem is relatively short, and visitors can expect to see history being made on a daily basis when they visit the "New Negro Metropolis." Painters such as Aaron Douglas are still creating eternal works; musicians Louis Armstrong and Duke Ellington are playing music that

Tips for Travelers

In-the-know visitors to Harlem always pick up a copy of the *Amsterdam News* for ten cents. This paper, started by James H. Anderson on 4 December 1909 with an initial investment of ten dollars, places particular emphasis on the social events within the community, including charity balls, concerts, and theatrical and art openings. With offices located in the heart of Harlem, and with a circulation of well over one hundred thousand, the paper also acts as a mouthpiece for the political concerns of one of the largest African American communities in the United States.

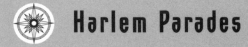

Harlem Parades

Visitors to Harlem, particularly those visiting in the spring and summer, might find themselves in the midst of a jubilant parade—or even participating in one. The following article from the *New York Times,* dated 24 August 1927, describes a typical summer spectacle in Harlem, this one hosted by the Negro Elks fraternal organization:

Under lowering skies and through intermittent showers, drenched but smiling and gaily clad Negro Elks marched [and danced] their way up Fifth Avenue from Sixty-first Street to Harlem yesterday afternoon in the four-hour parade of the Grand Lodge of the Improved Benevolent and Protective Order of Elks of the World. Assembling at 1 o'clock under the command of Grand Marshal Joseph Brown, members of 800 lodges from every state and many foreign countries fell into line with their twenty-five bands and passed perhaps 100,000 cheering onlookers, who lined the streets and crowded the windows of Harlem buildings, gay with bunting and banners of every description.

Woman Elk members, known as "Does," were almost as numerous as marchers of the other gender, while the leader of the women's band set the toes of marchers and bystanders tickling with the notes of "Charleston," "Ain't She Sweet," and "Me and My Shadow." A delegation of thirty Negro policemen from the West 135th Street station among the marchers received loud cheers and applause. White uniforms with purple trouser stripes and collars were the fashion for the men, though tuxedo coats and white flannels were also seen, with a heavy sprinkling of gold braid and brass buttons. One dignified group with top hats and cutaways followed a score of mounted policemen who were in the van. The women ran strongly to white and gold, with an occasional group in brown, cerise, purple and other colors.

Black Cross Nurses march in a Harlem parade celebrating opening day of the annual UNLA convention.

will resonate for generations to come; Zora Neale Hurston, Langston Hughes, and Countee Cullen continue to pen timeless classics.

In short, Harlem theaters, bookstores, and cafes are filled with living legends such as Du Bois, Hughes, and others who make take time to chat with curious tourists and new arrivals. For those of you visiting Harlem for the first time, you will be amazed when you cross the invisible border into this neighborhood. In his article, "Harlem: The Cultural Capital," James Weldon Johnson describes the astonishment experienced by those who visit the area today:

A stranger who rides up magnificent Seventh Avenue on a bus or in an automobile must be struck with surprise at the transformation which takes place after he crosses One Hundred and Twenty-fifth Street. Beginning here, the population suddenly darkens and he rides through twenty-five solid blocks where the passers-by, the shoppers, those sitting in restaurants, coming out of theaters, standing in doorways and looking out of windows are practically all Negroes; and then he emerges where the population as suddenly becomes white again. There is nothing just

W.E.B. Du Bois, founder of the NAACP, has written books that eloquently describe the pain and frustration of black people living in America.

like it in any other city in the country, for there is no preparation for it; no change in the character of the houses and streets; no change, indeed, in the appearance of the people, except for their color.[7]

Chapter 2

Harlem Basics

Harlem is a singing, dancing, good-time neighborhood that James Weldon Johnson describes in *Black Manhattan* as "exotic, colorful, and sensuous."[8] Simply walking down the broad, tree-lined Harlem streets may be as entertaining as visiting a restaurant or going to a dance club. With gorgeous homes to view on Strivers Row by day and rent parties happening almost every night, tourists on a budget can enjoy Harlem for only a few dollars a day. Be sure to bring your best clothes, however, because Harlem is a fashion-plate's paradise.

Getting to Harlem

Most travelers will arrive in New York City by train, beginning their Harlem odyssey at Forty-second Street and Park Avenue at Grand Central Station (the real name of which is Grand Central Terminal, since trains terminate their journey there). Built in 1913 for the staggering sum of $80 million, this majestic marble building with enormous gold-plated chandeliers hanging from its arched ceiling is sure to awe even the most jaded tourist.

Once inside Grand Central you need only to follow signs to the subway terminal inside the building, put a nickel in the turnstile slot, and walk down the stairs. The D, C, and A trains of the Independent Line come by every few minutes. Visitors in a hurry to get to Harlem will want the A train because, unlike the other two, this nonstop express train will take you directly to Harlem. As for what to expect, the following description by renowned Harlem Renaissance author Langston Hughes may help prepare you:

I can never put on paper the thrill of that underground ride to Harlem. I had never been in a subway before and it fascinated me—the noise, the speed, the green lights ahead. At every station I kept watching for the sign: 135TH STREET. When I saw it, I held my breath. I came out onto the platform with two heavy bags and looked around. It was still early morning and people were going to work. Hundreds of colored people! I wanted to shake hands with them, speak to them. I hadn't seen any colored people for so long. . . . I went up the steps and out into the

 # Speaking Harlemese

People not only look and act differently in Harlem, they also speak with a language all their own. Visitors might want to acquaint themselves with the slang, known as "Harlemese," so they will understand when the hep cats talk that jive:

Apple: New York City; the main stem is Harlem.
Barbecue: The girlfriend, a beauty.
Barrelhouse: Free and easy.
Beatup: Small change, as in "Can you lend me a little beatup?"
Bust your conk: Use your brain, apply yourself diligently.
Canary: Female vocalist in a jazz band.
Cat: A musician in a jazz band.
Collar: To get, to obtain, to comprehend: "I gotta collar me some food," or "Do your collar this jive?"
Drape: Suit of clothes, dress, costume.
Fews and two: Money or cash in small quantity.
Got your glasses on: You are ritzy or snooty; you fail to recognize your friends, you are upstage.
Gutbucket: Low-down, sad, slow, blues music.
Hep cat: A guy who knows all the answers, understands jive.
Igg: To ignore someone: "Don't igg me!"
Jive: Deception, phony and fake.
Lay your racket: To jive, to sell an idea, to promote a proposition.
Mitt pounding: Applause.
Murder: Something excellent or terrific: "That music is solid murder!"
Ofay: White person.
Riff: Hot lick, musical phrase.
Sailing: Intoxicated, high.
Salty: Angry, ill tempered.
Set of seven brights: Seven days, one week.
Togged to the bricks: Dressed to kill from head to foot.

Rail travelers in New York City arrive at majestic Grand Central Terminal, which offers tourists access to the Harlem-bound subway line.

bright September sunlight. Harlem! I stood there, dropped my bags, took a deep breath and felt happy again.[9]

Harlem's Three Major Streets

The Harlem neighborhood is served by two major streets, Lenox and Seventh Avenues, which run north and south. About midway through Harlem they are bisected by the east-west, 135th Street. Tourists wondering what sort of people

they might find on these three major streets only need to read the following description by celebrated novelist Rudolph Fisher from an article in the *Atlantic Monthly*:

Lenox Avenue is for the most part the boulevard of the [poor] unperfumed; "rats" they are often termed. Here, during certain hours, there is nothing unusual in the flashing of knives, the quick succession of pistol shots, the scream of a police-whistle or a woman.

But Seventh Avenue is the promenade of high-toned . . . strivers. It breathes a superior atmosphere, sings superior songs, laughs a superior laugh. Even were there no people, the difference would be clear: the middle of Lenox Avenue is adorned by street-car tracks, the middle of Seventh Avenue by [trees and grass].

A sunny afternoon finds locals and tourists on Lenox Avenue enjoying the sights and sounds of Harlem.

These two highways, frontiers of the opposed extreme of dark-skinned social life, are separated by an intermediate any-man's land, across which they communicate chiefly by way of 135th Street. Accordingly 135th Street is the heart and soul of black Harlem; it is common ground, the natural scene of unusual contacts, a region that disregards class. It neutralizes, equilibrates, binds, rescues union out of diversity.

In a fraction of a mile of 135th Street there occurs every institution necessary to civilization from a Carnegie Library opposite a public school at one to a police station beside an undertaker's parlor at another. But one institution outnumbers all others, an institution which, like the street itself, represents common ground: the barbershop.[10]

Harlem Neighborhoods

In addition to its major thoroughfares, Harlem is divided into several neighborhoods. The area originally called Washington Heights is among the most famous black neighborhoods in the United States. This district is located on the sloping hill from 145th Street to 155th Street between Amsterdam Avenue and Edgecombe Avenue. Today it is known far and wide as Sugar Hill, since it is associated with the "sweet life." Doorways to apartments here are watched over by doormen whose uniforms match the canopies above the sidewalk. This is an area where tourists might be lucky enough to get a glimpse of black celebrities going about their daily business. As *Ebony* magazine notes:

The most exciting facet of [visiting] Sugar Hill is knowing the big names which would stud its mailboxes and doorbells if Hill buildings only had such earthly things as mailboxes and doorbells. . . . Harlem's most talked-about men and women in law, sports, civil liberties, music, medicine, painting, business and literature live on Sugar Hill.[11]

Those who live atop the hill at 155th Street and Edgecombe look down —both physically and socially—on central Harlem, an area they call The Valley. While The Valley is home to most of the bookstores, theaters, clubs, restaurants, and studios that are central to the Harlem Renaissance, it is also where the poor live—and most crimes are committed.

The most dramatic building on Sugar Hill is the Colonial Parkway Apartments at 409 Edgecombe. Located on Coogan's Bluff high above the Harlem River, this thirteen-plus-story apartment house is the tallest in the neighborhood. It offers a commanding view of Colonial Park, the highway known as Harlem Speedway, and the Polo Grounds. The individual apartments within the building offer the most modern amenities, including dumbwaiters, electric refrigerators, tiled bathrooms, gas stoves, and two-passenger elevators staffed by uniformed operators.

The apartment with the most famous people is the five-acre Dunbar Apartments between 149th and 150th streets. This complex is home to Harlem's most respected residents, including W.E.B. Du Bois, Countee Cullen, renowned bandleader Fletcher Henderson, and actor and singer Paul Robeson.

Another exclusive, if less exciting, neighborhood is the Kingscourt Houses along West 138th and 139th Streets between Seventh and Eighth Avenues. Built in the early 1890s for well-to-do whites, the architecture alone makes this area worth a visit. But it is the people who live here today who put this neighborhood on the map. The distinguished red-hued row houses are filled with Harlem's so-called Talented Tenth, that is,

the 10 percent of the neighborhood residents that are successful doctors, lawyers, architects, musicians, writers, and others. Famous residents of the area today, whom a tourist might see strolling on a Saturday night, include prizefighter Harry Wills; comedian and movie star Stepin Fetchit; jazz pianist Eubie Blake; W.C. Handy, father of the blues; and Vertner Tandy, the first black architect to be licensed in New York State.

Living in this neighborhood is a measure of one's success. When poor and middle-class blacks in Harlem noted how strenuously the black elite strived to emulate the rich white folks who once lived in the Kingscourt Houses, they called the area Strivers Row, a name that stuck.

Cheap Accommodations

Not all residents of Strivers Row and Sugar Hill are wealthy, however, and many make

The huge Dunbar Apartments complex is home to some of Harlem's most famous residents, including Paul Robeson and W.E.B. Du Bois.

ends meet the same way people do down in The Valley—by taking in boarders who can rent beds by the night, week, or month. While this type of lodging is usually inexpensive—one or two dollars a night, do not expect much in the way of amenities if you chose to sojourn in this manner.

In the better neighborhoods such accommodations might feature one's own room, some with a private bath. In The Valley, boarding rooms are often found in long narrow apartments called "railroad flats" where a "bedroom" might be nothing more than a corner of living room cordoned off by flimsy sheets hanging from the ceiling. While this offers a little privacy, some folks simply rent out a couch or daybed in the middle of the living room, sometimes by the hour. Do not be surprised if, upon rising in the morning, another guest immediately takes your place on the mattress. While these conditions might not be ideal, it is a way to make friends and meet people. It is advised, however, that you keep your valuables in your possession at all times, even sleeping with them under your pillow if you are doubtful about your "roommates." Those wishing to find such rooms should look for signs in windows or doorways, or advertisements on bulletin boards or in newspapers.

"Niggerati Manor"

The cheapest accommodations in Harlem are free, but they are only open to artists and writers. These rent-free rooms are located at 267 West 136th Street in a building known as the "267 House" but jokingly referred to as "Niggerati Manor" by Zora Neale Hurston (a twist on the term "literati," or literary intellectuals). Noted residents include painters Bruce Nugent and novelist Wallace Thurman. While vacancies are, understandably, in short supply, those "freelance bohemians" with the wherewithal to compete with Harlem's literati may be lucky enough to be offered boarding at the 267 House. Lodging here is not for the conservative, sober, or faint of heart, however. As Theophilus Lewis writes in his "Harlem Sketchbook" column in the *Amsterdam News*:

The story goes out that the bathtubs in the house [are] always packed with sourmash [whiskey], while gin [flows] from all the water taps and the flush boxes [behind the toilets are] filled with . . . beer . . . In the case of Niggerati Manor, a great deal more smoke [comes] out of the windows than [is] warranted by the size of the fire in the [furnace].[12]

Other Accommodations

Travelers who desire more traditional lodging can stay in some of the boarding houses and hotels. Perhaps the most famous boarding house is owned by Lottie Joplin. She is the wife of Scott Joplin, the pianist whose compositions such as "Maple Leaf Rag" made ragtime music an international fad in the late 1800s

Travelers on a budget can rent inexpensive rooms at the YMCA. During the summer months, reservations are a must.

while providing a cornerstone for jazz. Joplin's Boarding House, at 251 131st Street, caters mostly to entertainers. Famous guests have included jazz pianists Jelly Roll Morton and Willie "The Lion" Smith.

One of the best hotels in Harlem is the Hotel Olga on the southwest corner of West 145th

Tips for Travelers: The Harlem YMCA

The Harlem YMCA, 180 West 135th Street, was opened in 1919 as the black population growth was booming. The Harlem "Y" offers recreational facilities as well as vocational classes, lectures, theatrical and musical performances, and community meetings. It is also a center of political activity. Tourists can rent rooms at the Y for a few dollars a night, joining the company of such famous luminaries as poets Claude McKay and Langston Hughes who temporarily lived at the Y. It should be noted that vacancies are often scarce, especially during the summer. Call ahead for reservations.

Street and Lenox. The hotel is small with limited accommodations on only two floors. Rooms rent for a reasonable two to three dollars per night. Despite this fact the Olga is often a destination for Alain Locke, and to Nancy Cunard, millionaire heiress to the Cunard Shipping Lines whose relationship with black musician Henry Crowder has made frequent headlines in the tabloid press.

Millionaire heiress Nancy Cunard is spotted in Harlem with two male companions, including jazz pianist Henry Crowder (right).

Inexpensive Entertainment: Rent Parties

The housing shortage in Harlem has resulted in rents that are anywhere from ten to thirty dollars higher than they are in white neighborhoods. Since African Americans are also paid less, many have had a difficult time making the rent every month. Fortunately fun is free, and Harlem residents have figured out a way to make ends meet by throwing "rent parties." Eating, drinking, and dancing is the order of the day (or night) at rent party gatherings, which are open to anyone—friends and strangers alike—who will contribute ten to fifty cents toward the host's rent. Tourists wishing to meet colorful neighborhood characters, learn about "real life" in Harlem, and find out the latest dance steps should try to attend a rent party or two while visiting the neighborhood.

Rent parties may be thrown any night of the week, but most often take place on Saturday nights or Thursdays, when many maids, butlers, and other domestics have the night off. The festivities are advertised on cards that are handed out by hosts on street corners or at pool halls, laundromats, and speakeasies. These cards often contain catchy slogans meant to attract guests, such as:

You don't get nothing
   for being an angel
   child,
So you might as well
   get real busy and
   get real wild.[13]

Live music comes in a variety of forms, from single piano players to five piece jazz bands, depending on the party. Slow dances feature men sensually "slow-dragging" women around the cleared living room floor. Peppier numbers will find everyone doing the most popular dances such as the Charleston or the Black Bottom. Sometimes dance contests are held with the prize being a bottle of whiskey or a few dollars from the donation bucket.

Rent party food is from the school of southern "soul" cooking, with such delicacies as "Hopping John" (rice and black-eyed peas), rice and chicken feet, chitterlings, okra gumbo, pig feet and sauerkraut, sweet potato pone, and hog maws.

Of course no rent party would be successful unless liquor was flowing freely. Guests can expect to find beer, whiskey, wine, and that bootleg liquor cooked up in the bathroom known as bathtub gin.

A Harlem couple demonstrates their sophisticated dancing style during a romantic number at a popular nightclub.

Sometimes side rooms contain other illegal entertainments such as strippers, prostitutes, and gambling. In the wee hours, professional musicians, fresh from gigs, might show up and jam until dawn.

Whatever the entertainment, the party is successful as long as the rent gets paid. Those who fail to satisfy their landlords will find their belongings hauled out to the sidewalk the next day.

What to Wear

The latest Harlem fashions may be seen at rent parties, or anywhere else visitors travel. Things are less formal during the day, of course, as cooks, factory workers, laundresses, and cabbies can be seen on 125th and Lenox in their drab work clothes. At night, however, tourists should be aware that the sidewalks of Harlem are transformed by high fashion. For men, white spats, striped pants, black brogues, velvet-collared overcoats, and walking sticks are the order of the day (or night). These clothes can be obtained at the expensive Schwartz and Harrison Emporium on Seventh Avenue, a place whose customers the *Amsterdam News* refers to as "black sheiks with footlight aspirations."[14]

Ladies are often seen in the latest flapper fashions. Influenced by European designers, these include small helmetlike cloche hats, short dresses, made-up faces, silk stockings, short, straightened hair, and long strings of beads. Even respectable women of fashion have been seen wearing unbuckled galoshes that "flap" when they walk, hence the name flappers. Exotic monkey-fur-collared coats, and hats with egret feathers, are seen on those who can afford such luxuries.

After church on Sundays, Seventh between 125th and 138th Streets turns into a fashion parade as families stroll the avenue. Many a visitor to Harlem is happily astounded by this activity, seen with such intensity nowhere else in the United States. Johnson describes what tourists can expect to see while strolling in Harlem:

Strolling in Harlem does not mean merely walking along Lenox or upper Seventh Avenue or One Hundred and Thirty-fifth Street; it means that those streets are places for socializing. One puts on one's best clothes and fares forth to pass the time pleasantly with the friends and acquaintances and, most important of all, the strangers he is sure of meeting. One saunters along, he hails this one, exchanges a word or two with that one, stops for a short chat with the other one. He comes up to a laughing, chattering group, in which he may have only one friend or acquaintance, but that gives him the privilege of joining in. He does join in and takes part in the joking, the small talk and gossip, and makes new acquaintances.

He passes on and arrives in front of one of the theatres, studies the bill for a while, undecided about going in. He finally moves on a few steps farther and joins another group and is introduced to two or three pretty girls who have just come to Harlem, perhaps only for a visit; and finds a reason to be glad that he postponed going into the theatre. The hours of a summer evening run by rapidly. This is not simply going out for a walk; it is more like going out for adventure.[15]

While strolling, women show off their fur coats, feather boas, and colorful shawls while twirling parasols. Men strut in black suits, white spats, and silk hats. While this procession has been compared to the Easter display by white people on the exclusive Fifth Avenue, spectacle in Harlem happens every Sunday. As Fisher writes in *The Walls of Jericho*: "Indeed, even Fifth Avenue on Easter never quite attains this; practice makes perfect, and Harlem's Seventh Avenue boasts fifty-two Easters a year."[16]

Churches

Much like the display on Seventh Avenue, the churches of Harlem are crowded not just on Easter but every Sunday. And block-for-block Harlem probably has more churches than any other neighborhood in New York. Johnson estimates that there are "something like one hundred and sixty colored churches in Harlem. . . . A hundred of these could be closed and there would be left a sufficient number

to supply the religious needs of the community."[17] Most of these houses of worship are storefront churches that might be housed in a former candy store or shoe store or the dusty basement of a tenement apartment.

Like most other events in Harlem, church services are conducted with drama and style unseen elsewhere. And since many of the storefront worshipers are poor and from the South, they are

Harlem's numerous churches, from modest storefront buildings to the most impressive structures, are full every Sunday. Tourists are welcome to attend church services.

not interested in the calm proceedings at the larger, more established churches. Civil rights leader Bayard Rustin explains that these are people who are "used to screaming and yelling at services, rolling in the aisles, and speaking in tongues."[18]

Those who prefer their religious services a tad less exciting can attend the Mother AME Zion Church, the oldest black church in New York State, founded in 1796. During the years of slavery,

Mother Zion was a "Freedom Church" on the Underground Railroad where escaped slaves were hidden, fed, clothed, and cared for. The Neo-Gothic Church, at 136th Street between Lenox and Seventh, was completed in 1925.

Other major Harlem churches include St. Mark's AME on 138th and St. Nicholas, the Abyssinian Baptist at 138th and Lenox, and St. Philip's Episcopal, known as the "Richest Negro Church in America, 204 West 134th Street."

The Dancing Evangelist

The following article by shipping heiress Nancy Cunard describes the scene at a service at the Salem Methodist on Seventh Avenue with Reverend George Becton, known as the "Dancing Evangelist." These red-hot religious revivals are open to all, and any visitor to Harlem would do well to attend one while in the neighborhood:

When we got into the [church] a very large audience was waiting for the "Dancing Evangelist" (that is Becton's title, because of his terrific physical activity). A group of "sisters" all in white spread itself fan-wise in the balcony. There was a concert stage with deacons and some of Becton's 12 disciples, and the 7 or 8 absolutely first-class musicians who compose the orchestra. . . . Nothing like a church, an evening concert. The music starts, a deep-toned Bach piece, then . . . the long spirituals . . . the audience, answers back. They begin to beat time with their feet too. The "spirit" is coming with the volume of

sound. At this point Becton enters quietly, stands silent on the stage. . . . How do [the parishioners] reconcile Becton's exquisite smartness (pearl-grey suit, top hat, cane, ivory gloves, his youthful look and lovely figure), the whole sparkle about him, with the customary ponderousness of the other drab men of God? A sophisticated audience? No, for they appear to be mainly domestic workers, small shop workers, old and young, an evidently religious public, and one or two whites. A new spiritual has begun; the singing gets intenser, foot-beating all around now, bodies swaying, and clapping of hands in unison. Now and again a voice, several voices, rise above the rest in a single phrase, the footbeat becomes a stamp. . . . Far away in the audience a woman gets "seized," leaps up and down on the same spot. . . . At one moment I counted ten women in this same violent trance, not two with the same gestures, yet all in rhythm, half-time or double time.

The Salem Methodist Church on 129th and Seventh was the site of last year's celebrated wedding between poet Countee Cullen and Yolanda Du Bois, daughter of W.E.B. Du Bois. On April 9, 1928, more than five thousand people jammed the streets around the church attempting to attend this wedding between Harlem Renaissance "royalty." As Mr. Du Bois wrote: "It was the symbolic march of young and black America . . . it was a new race, a new thought, a new thing rejoicing in a ceremony as old as the world."[19]

However, the marriage lasted little longer than the ceremony. Cullen quickly left for Paris with a male companion while Yolanda remained infatuated with jazz musician Jimmie Junceford. The couple were soon divorced.

Tourists should be aware that church going in Harlem can be an all-day and all-night affair. Most of the large institutions open early on Sunday and stay open until eleven o'clock at night. The churches are never empty during these long hours, and hot meals are served by special committees so that people do not have to leave.

A World of Contradictions

Like the famous marriage between Cullen and Du Bois, Harlem is a world of contradictions. Visitors can attend church services with devout worshipers, then drink bootleg whiskey with those very same people at a rent party the next night. The aura of pomp and pageantry on display in Sugar Hill can be quickly deflated when one hears a finely dressed gentleman speaking "Harlemese." And grinding poverty and despair can be found a short stroll from Strivers Row. That, however, is Harlem today. No matter where you are from—north, south, east, or west—you will be sure to see sights and experience delights unique in the world today. And whether you say it in plain English or Harlemese, "that ain't no jive."

Chapter 3

Eating and Drinking and Gambling in Harlem

Eating and drinking in Harlem can be like taking a culinary trip around the world. In the three square miles between 125th and 135th Streets, and between Lenox and Seventh Avenues, more than 125 entertainment places are serving both black and white clientele. There are speakeasies, cellars, lounges, cafés, taverns, supper clubs, rib joints, and numerous bars and grills.

High Society

Since the mid-1920s, with the popularity of all-black music revues such as *Shuffle Along* on Broadway, the formerly black character of Harlem has changed with the influx of whites from downtown. And the Caucasians who travel to Harlem are not your average Americans. In fact many who have been afflicted by "Harlemania," a nearly hysterical love of the neighborhood, are members of international high society. Among those arriving in their Stutz and Daimler touring cars are Gertrude Vanderbilt Whitney, granddaughter of railroad magnate Cornelius Vanderbilt; French princess Violette Murat; German-born financier Otto Kahn; movie star Harold Lloyd; actress Beatrice Lillie; torch singer Libby Holman; and Lady Patricia Mountbatten, wife of British naval commander Lord Mountbatten. These people may be observed in expensive restaurants, or at "low-down" speakeasies when they want to go "slumming."

Of course, there is a negative side to all this attention from high society. Blacks are barred from several of the best restaurants, where only the wait-staff and entertainers are black. And racial stereotypes prevail, as film star, comedian, and frequent visitor to Harlem, Jimmy Durante, says:

> You sort of go primitive [in Harlem] . . . with bands moaning the blues like [nobody's] business, slim bare-thighed brown-skin gals tossing their torsos, and the Negro melody artists bearing down something terrible on the [blues] notes. . . . [But the] average colored man you see along the streets in Harlem doesn't know any more about these dumps than the old maid in North Forks, South Dakota.[20]

Expensive Dining

While average visitors may be shut out of the fanciest restaurants, many cater to any black and white patrons who can afford to pay the steep prices of a meal. In these exclusive "black and tan" bistros, diners can easily spend twenty-five dollars or more per person. On Sugar Hill, Craig's Colony Club on St. Nicholas Place attracts a gourmet crowd interested in prime rib and seafood. The black-and-tan elite meet to eat at the Fatman's Bar-and-Grill on 155th Street. Here tourists can rub elbows with bandleaders Duke Ellington, Artie Shaw, and Jimmy Dorsey, as well as singing legends Cab Calloway and Maxine Sullivan, and actress Tallulah Bankhead.

Folks from Strivers Row and Sugar Hill often journey to 388 Lenox to the

A traveling party poses in their elegant Stutz touring car. Wealthy white patrons from all over the world frequent Harlem night spots.

Tourists with gourmet tastes may spot well-known musicians like Duke Ellington (pictured) dining at Craig's Colony Club on swanky Sugar Hill.

Club Harlem African Room, which bills itself as the "Favorite Retreat for the Select and Elite."

Reasonably Priced Food

More reasonable prices—and a relaxed, casual atmosphere—may be found at Tabbs, located at 140th Street and Lenox. This place serves a chicken dinner popular with longtime residents in the neighborhood. Ragtime music serenades diners in the back part of the restaurant known as the Grill Room.

For about two dollars a person, the Marguerite, on 132nd between Lenox and Seventh, lives up to its motto and "guarantees you a full stomach."[21]

Those who wish to drink fine, imported Italian wine with their dinners should visit La Rosa on Seventh near 139th Street. Other Italian delicacies are served at the Venetian Tea Room on 135th between Seventh and Eighth Avenues.

Visitors homesick for southern cooking such as chitterlings and biscuits and gravy can get some down-home dinners at the Blue Grass on 130th Street and Seventh.

Those on a shoestring budget can easily find a number of moderately priced, casual restaurants offering excellent fare.

Food and Music

If you like music while you eat, Harlem offers many choices. One popular hang-out on 135th is Teddy's Place, described by Fisher:

Teddy's [Place] . . . stays open all night and draws all manner of men and women by the common appeal of good food. Oddly, it was once a mere barroom lunch, and the mahogany bar-counter still serves the majority of Teddy's patrons, those who are content to sit upon stools and rub elbows with anybody. But there is now a back room also, with a side entrance available from the street. Here there are round-top tables beside the walls, and here parties with ladies may be more elegantly served. It is really a "high-class" grill-room, and its relation to the bar-counter lunch-room, the whole situated on democratic 135th

Street, marks Teddy a man of considerable business acumen.

In one corner of the grill-room there is an excellent phonograph which plays a record repeatedly without changing. A song ends; you wait a few moments while the instrument is automatically re-wound and adjusted; and the song begins again.[22]

If the phonograph seems a little old-fashioned to you, venture over to The Barbecue at 131st Street and Seventh. This place, located upstairs from the famous Connie's Inn jazz club, features some of the hottest new jazz records on their famous jukebox, in which songs can be played for a nickel each. In addition to its swinging tunes, The Barbecue is considered the best rib joint in Harlem.

Those wishing for more rowdy entertainment should go over to the dining and dancing district known as "Jungle Alley" on 133rd Street between Lenox and Seventh. Here The Clam House offers seafood and the singing entertainment of the "torrid warbler,"

Tips for Travelers

If these restaurants are beyond your budget, or you want a snack, the cheapest eats of all can be found at stands called "coffee pots" that are located on nearly every corner. These stands offer basic coffee, rolls, and pie for those on the run or with only a few quarters in their pockets.

Gladys Bentley, the 250-pound vocalist who sings bawdy songs while wearing a top hat and tails. If you need further inspiration to catch her act, ponder a review of her music by Langston Hughes:

Miss Bentley [sits and plays] a big piano all night long, literally all night, without stopping—singing songs like "The St. James Infirmary," from ten in the evening until dawn, with scarcely a break between the notes, sliding from one song to another, with a powerful and continuous underbeat of jungle rhythm. Miss Bentley [shows] an amazing exhibition of musical energy—a large, dark, masculine lady, whose feet [pound] the floor while her fingers [pound] the keyboard— a perfect piece of African sculpture, animated by her own rhythm.[23]

While the musical entertainment is not as good at Ed Small's Paradise, the choreography is certainly interesting. Ed's, the most prestigious club owned by African Americans, features singing and dancing waiters who dance the Charleston as they maneuver between the tables. All the while they stylishly spin their empty trays on one finger. Several extratalented waiters can even spin their trays, albeit slowly, while laden with drinks.

Chinese Cuisine

Several popular Harlem restaurants offer exotic taste treats for those who are tired

Ed Small's Paradise, a chic club owned by African Americans, is a key attraction. Professional dancers perform here nightly, but the dancing waiters frequently steal the show.

of fried chicken and other common dishes. The Oriental on 136th Street combines flavors of Chinese and African American cuisine. The Oriental occupies an entire three-story house where the floors are thickly carpeted and linen-clad tables fill the rooms. Tea is served along with Chinese specialties, while a solo piano player entertains with jazz music in the main dining room. On some nights entertainment is provided by a singer, described by Fisher as "a slender little 'brown' [girl] with a voice of silver and a way of singing a song that [makes] you forget your food."[24]

Members of the Talented Tenth can be seen at the Oriental on any given night. Songwriters Henry Creamer and Turner Layton, of "After You've Gone" and "Strut Miss Lizzie" fame, are regular patrons, as are preacher Harry Bragg and actor Paul Robeson.

Tips for Travelers: Alcohol Is Still Illegal!

V isitors from other parts of the nation might be shocked to see the flagrant consumption of illegal alcoholic beverages in Harlem. In fact, a survey by the *Amsterdam News* found that proprietors at one out of every seven cigar stores, lunchrooms, and beauty parlors are selling illegal booze. Although it would be nearly impossible to eat and dance in Harlem without visiting "speaks" or other joints where alcohol is found, the stuff remains illegal. While it is generally assumed police are paid to look the other way, if a patrolman wanted to arrest you for any reason, a pint of gin would certainly provide an excuse. If this happens you might find yourself locked up in Harlem's 38th Police Precinct jail facing a stiff fine or even looking at prison time. While this guide recommends that you avoid drinking at all, if you choose to drink, be very careful.

The Bamboo Inn is another highly regarded Chinese restaurant. Located at 2389 Seventh Avenue, this eatery has a balcony and mirrored ball over its dance floor. The Bamboo is pricey, however, and average tourists might feel out of place there. Author Wallace Thurman described the clientele as "Well-dressed men escorting expensively garbed women and girls; models from *Vanity Fair* [magazine] with brown, yellow, and black skins. Doctors, lawyers, [businessmen] and their ladies with fine manners . . . fine clothes and fine houses to return to when the night's fun has ended."[25]

Speakeasies for the Working Class

If you are one of the many visitors to Harlem who cannot afford the extravagant prices of the Bamboo Inn or the Fatman's, take heart. On the side streets around Jungle Alley, the working-class crowd, both black and tan, can find food and drink at rock-bottom prices. Of course you get what you pay for, and tourists should be aware that many of these "low-down" joints can be dangerous. Keep your cash in a money belt, leave your expensive jewelry locked up at the hotel, and do not flash large bills.

Police estimate that on every square block around Jungle Alley there are least ten cheap speakeasies, known as "lap joints" because prostitutes are often seen sitting on the laps of male customers. The Sugar Cane at 135th and Fifth Avenue is typical of these low-down joints. To gain entry you must first satisfy the doorman that you are not a police officer. If he thinks you are all right, he will ring a bell and a shutter in the door will open. The doorman will give the bouncer the OK and instruct him to pull back a large bolt and chain connected to the inner door.

Inside you will find a dimly lit, steep flight of stairs that leads down to a narrow, unfinished basement about 25 feet wide and 125 feet long. The floor is covered in sawdust, and the thick smoke of cheap cigarettes and cigars fills the air. On weeknights about one hundred people will be gathered in various states of drunkenness. On a Saturday night expect about twice that many. A few white faces can be seen among the black customers who are mostly working folks— maids, bootblacks, stevedores, cabbies, and the like.

Folks are seated in wooden café chairs around several dozen wobbly wooden tables. If you order a drink do not be fooled by the labels on the bottles. Although they may say they are filled with fine liquor such as Hennessy or Cutty Sark, the bottles are really filled with cheap bootleg booze. Of course the prices are less than 50 percent of what you might pay for the real thing, so few complain. The most popular drink, and one that was invented in Harlem, is called a "shorty." The name is misleading, however: A shorty contains a "double-double," or four shots of liquor. Too many shortys might send you sailing and give you a terrible hangover the next day.

Locals dance the night away at a neighborhood nightclub. The occasional white face may be seen in such establishments.

Another drink you might want to avoid is known simply as "smoke." This stuff promises to make a "wildcat out of a mouse,"[26] but beware. Brewed in the Bowery, New York's poorest and toughest neighborhood, this stuff is grain alcohol cut with water. Although it is only fifteen cents a drink, it might turn you *from* a wildcat *into* a mouse and leave you crawling around on the floor. If you pass out from smoke, you might wake up without your ring, wallet, or money clip. Then you would be known as a sucker, or *spruce* in Harlemese.

Speakeasy Entertainment

Like nearly every other Harlem establishment, The Sugar Cane features a jazz or blues band, usually with a female "torch" singer crying out lovelorn blues or up-tempo jazz numbers. Colored lightbulbs of blue and red hang above couples twirling on the dance floor; if it becomes too crowded, people simply shuffle their feet, or "dance on a dime."

As the night wears on, expect the noise level to grow with the level of inebriation. Those who can hang on until 3 A.M. will witness an influx of fresh faces as the city's licensed cabarets close down due to New York's curfew laws, forcing partygoers to the illegal speakeasies. If you are lucky enough to be there on a good night, you might see professional musicians and dancers doing their acts in exchange for burgers and booze. On one recent night,

Friends raise their glasses in a toast at the Cotton Club, one of Harlem's most famous night spots.

The Caucasian Invasion

Visitors returning to Harlem after a several-year absence will notice that many restaurants and speakeasies that formerly catered to blacks only are now packed with white customers. With the mid-decade success of black authors, jazz musicians, and actors, white people have been flooding into Harlem in unprecedented numbers. Some old hangouts are even turning away the black customers who helped make them successful in the first place. This "Caucasian Invasion" has changed the face of the neighborhood, much to the dismay of visitors such as renowned author Rudolph Fisher, who describes returning to his favorite club in 1927 after living in Washington, D.C., for five years:

I remembered one place especially where my own crowd used to hold forth; and, hoping to find some old-timers there still, I sought it out one midnight. The old, familiar [piano playing] plunkety-plunk wel-comed me from below as I entered. I descended the same old narrow stairs, came into the same smoke-misty basement, and found myself a chair at one of the ancient white porcelain, mirror-smooth tables. I drew a deep breath and looked about, seeking familiar faces. "What a lot of 'fays!' [white people]" I thought, as I noticed the number of white guests. Presently I grew puzzled and began to stare, then I gaped—and gasped. I found myself wondering if this was the right place—if, indeed, this was Harlem at all. I suddenly became aware that, except for the waiters and members of the orchestra, I was the only Negro in the place.

After a while I left it and wandered about in a daze from night-club to night-club . . . . There was no mistake; my discovery was real and was repeatedly confirmed. . . . The best of Harlem's black cabarets have changed their names and turned white.

for example, the dancing Bon Ton Buddies showed up to do their dance routine from the Broadway musical revue *Hot Chocolates*.

During such performances patrons are expected to toss crumpled dollar bills at the dancers while pounding the tables with their glasses. Such revelries continue until 7 A.M. when the whistles blow on nearby factories—a shrill reminder that another busy New York day is about to begin.

Those who want to alter their consciousness yet stay legal use marijuana.

Marijuana cigarettes, or reefers, are sold on the street for ten cents apiece around Jungle Alley, and Harlem tourists often see people smoking around speaks, dance clubs, and other places of entertainment.

One area where you should be extremely careful is the Fifth Avenue district between 132nd and 138th Streets. This area, known as "Coke Village," is notorious for its cocaine dealers and prostitutes. Called the "hottest sector for vice in Harlem"[27] by the *Amsterdam News*, it is often patronized by rich white folk looking for "hop" and whores.

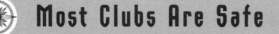

Most Clubs Are Safe

Most Harlem nightclubs are perfectly safe, as James Weldon Johnson informs tourists in *Black Manhattan:*

To many . . . a Harlem night-club is a den of iniquity, where the Devil holds high revel. The fact is that the average night-club is as orderly as many a Sunday-school picnic has been. These clubs are patronized by many quite respectable citizens. Anyone who visits them expecting to be shocked is likely to be disappointed. Generally nightclubbers go simply to have a good time. They laugh and talk and they dance to the most exhilarating music. And they watch a first-rate review. Certainly there are infractions of [Prohibition laws]; but they also take place in the best-regulated homes.

Most Harlem nightclubs are respectable establishments. Here, couples dance to the music of Cab Calloway's band at the Cotton Club on New Year's Eve.

Gambling and the Numbers

Gambling is another popular—if illegal—pastime in Harlem. In fact a staggering $30 million is spent annually by neighborhood residents playing "the numbers." To play this game bettors pick a three-digit number between 000 and 999. The winning number is linked to financial figures generated by the New York Stock Exchange every day. (They are, from the right, the seventh and eighth digits of the closing number on the stock exchange plus the seventh digit of the balances.) For a one-dollar bet you have a one-in-one-thousand chance of winning six hundred dollars. If you are not a high roller, numbers is the only game in which you can bet a single penny. If it is a lucky penny you can win one dollar.

Those who bet the numbers seem to be on a constant search for lucky numbers, betting digits that coincide with birthdays, addresses, laundry tickets, and even shoe and hat sizes.

Numbers betting often takes place in eating and drinking establishments where it is controlled by the same mobsters who fill the bars with illegal liquor. Numbers "kings" and "queens" take bets out in the open. If you want to participate, just look for the well-dressed man or woman walking through the crowds, smiling and greeting people. (Their smiles are a result of the 10 percent cut they make on all the bets they collect every day.) Booklets on how to play the numbers are available almost everywhere, authored by people with names such as Prince Ali, Madame Fu Futtam, Professor Konje, and the Red Witch. Hot numbers are peddled to people in bars and restaurants, often for a small price. Sometimes they are sold with incense or bottles of allegedly magical oil to be used while praying before making a bet.

Satisfy Your Every Appetite

Gambling, drinking, and eating are central to social life in Harlem today. Whether you want to hit the numbers, swill some bathtub gin, or simply have a down-home fried chicken dinner, you can hardly go wrong in Harlem. With so many restaurants and speakeasies to see on nearly every block, you can keep on the move and try new joints every day or every hour. Whatever your taste, however heavy your wallet, no matter what the time of day, there is always a place in Harlem to satisfy your every appetite.

Chapter 4

Jazz and Dance in Harlem

Nightlife in Harlem revolves around jazz, a musical style that was born in New Orleans, grew up in Chicago, and came of age in New York City. Begun as a musical style that combined elements of ragtime, blues, black spirituals, and European marching bands, jazz is a sound invented by African Americans and unique to the United States. Marked by a syncopated rhythm that lends itself to dancing, and an improvised style where musicians make up "riffs" as they play, jazz bursts forth from record players and radios nearly everywhere in Harlem.

Although jazz was first played around the turn of the century, New York did not have much of a jazz scene until the 1920s. With the popularity of the Harlem Renaissance, musicians began to flood into Harlem from Kansas City, Chicago, New Orleans, and other points south and west. The combined force of these hundreds of itinerant musicians can be seen—and heard—in nearly every street and alley in Harlem. Improvised music emanates from restaurants, speakeasies, bookstores, apartment stoops, and street corners.

This music has also wafted downtown to the white neighborhoods where thousands of upper-class New Yorkers are buying jazz records and traveling uptown to patronize black jazz clubs. Some are even learning jazz dance in "colored dance" studios located throughout Harlem.

Jazz Club Ambiance
Harlem swings with the sounds of jazz seven nights a week. As Johnson writes:

A visit to Harlem at night—the principal streets [are] never deserted, [festive] crowds skipping from one place of amusement to another, lines of taxicabs and limousines standing under the sparkling lights of the entrances to famous nightclubs, the subway kiosks swallowing and disgorging crowds all night long—gives the impression that Harlem never sleeps and that the inhabitants thereof [rely on] jazz [for their very] existence.[28]

Jazz-loving Harlem tourists can choose from nearly fifteen major jazz bands—and one hundred lesser-known ensembles—that all play locally. The groups can be heard at a variety of clubs with different names but with similar ambiance.

In addition, the *Amsterdam News* states that: "Harlem has 300 girl dancers continually working in the joints. About 800 are always ready for an audition, of any sort. It has 150 boys, perhaps the best aggregation of tap and buck dancers extant. But 1,500 young men claim professional standing as dancers."[29]

Tourists can expect the typical Harlem jazz club to consist of a crowded room where loud conversations and

Harlem nightclubs draw from a talent pool of over two thousand professional dancers, although fewer than five hundred are employed on any given evening.

liquor-lubricated laughter ricochet through the air. Nicer clubs are decorated with mirrors, fine wood paneling, and linen-covered dining tables, while down-at-the-heels rooms might have a hodgepodge of mismatched chairs, cheap framed prints, and rickety wooden tables. Do not let the atmosphere fool you, however. Even the tawdriest bar can have a skilled "stride" piano player who uses his left hand to play percussive, "striding" bass notes while his right hand "tickles" out the melody on the upper keys. The keyboardists call themselves "ticklers," but they have given each other rowdy nicknames such as "The Bear," "The Beetle," "The Beast," and "The Brute" that accurately portray their prowess on the piano. Harlem's most famous ticklers are Willie "The Lion" Smith, Ferdinand "Jelly Roll" Morton, and Thomas "Fats" Waller.

Larger clubs usually feature a multipiece band, the size—and talent—of which is often in direct proportion to the amount of money carried by the gents in the audience. Clubs for the poor and working classes may feature a trumpet, drummer, bassist, guitarist, and saxophone player playing jazz standards.

No savvy tourist will leave Harlem without seeing famed "stride" pianists "Jelly Roll" Morton (top) and Fats Waller perform.

Tourists should be aware that these bands are paid by customers' tips. You are expected to place anywhere from 15 to 20 percent of your drink tab in the bowl or cigar box on a table in the center of the room. In addition, those throwing a few greenback dollars into the tip box will notice a marked improvement in the quality of the music.

Sometimes these boxes can cause trouble, however. The great stride pianist, Willie "The Lion" Smith, has had to have a mirror installed over his piano so he can keep an eye on the tip box as he plays. Apparently musicians, customers, and waiters are known to help themselves to The Lion's share.

Clubs that cater to wealthier clientele feature the world-class entertainment of Fletcher Henderson, Duke Ellington, Louis Armstrong, or dozens of other hit makers whose records are in high demand today.

Where to Go

A cabaret known as the Oriental on 135th Street and Lenox (not to be confused with the Oriental Restaurant on 136th) is typical of the clubs today in Harlem. Fisher's description of the Oriental, along with its entertainment,

Wealthy clientele frequent clubs featuring first-rate bands like the renowned jazz ensemble led by pianist Fletcher Henderson (fifth from left).

Duke Ellington and his famous band fairly percolate with energy and sophistication.

provides a vivid picture of the place for tourists who might wish to visit there:

> An upstairs place, it [is] nevertheless as dingy as any of the cellars, and the music fairly [fights] its way through the babble and smoke to one's ears, suffering in transit weird and incredible distortion. The prize pet here [is] a slim, little lad, unbelievably black beneath his high-brown powder [makeup], wearing a Mexican bandit costume with a bright-colored headdress and sash. I see him now, poor kid, in all his glory, shimmying for enraptured women, who marveled at the perfect control of his voluntary abdominal tremors. He used to let the women reach out and put their hands on his sash to palpate those tremors—for a quarter.[30]

Those who desire less risqué entertainment might walk over to the Garden of Joy, an open-air cabaret on Seventh Avenue between 138th and 139th Streets. This place has a large, wooden dance floor. Hanging above the cabaret, and looking like a lampshade, a canvas roof is supported by poles. The Garden of Joy is located near the Abyssinian Church and in the summer, when the church holds its festive camp meetings outdoors in a large circus tent, the high-intensity spirituals of the choir mix curiously with the raucous blues and jazz emanating from the cabaret.

The Savoy

The Savoy, which covers an entire city block on Lenox Avenue between 140th and 141st Streets, is in a class by itself. Opened in March 1926 at a cost of a startling two hundred thousand dollars, this "dance palace" is a community ballroom where black people, rich or poor, local or tourist, can gain admission to jazz heaven for only fifty cents on most nights and seventy-five cents on Sundays. The Savoy also readily accepts white customers, and in this way has helped introduce the sounds of black America to a wider audience.

The Savoy is an architectural wonder, with a spacious lobby crowned with a cut-glass chandelier. The block-long dance hall, atop two dazzling mirror-lined, marble staircases, can hold up to four thousand people—as it often does on Friday and Saturday nights. The Savoy employs two bands at once so that

The Harlem Renaissance Basketball Club

While most Harlem clubs only feature music and dancing, you might be able to catch a basketball game at the Renaissance Casino Ballroom on 2351 Seventh Avenue. This ballroom is home to the Harlem Renaissance Basketball Club, a team that plays its home games on the dance floor. The "Rens," founded in 1923 by club owner Robert Douglas, are the first all-black sports team in the United States. They came together to play in response to the racism that prevents African American athletes from playing on white teams.

Their first professional game, on 30 November 1923, was a victory over the Collegiate Big Five at 28–22. In the following years the Rens came to be known as the best basketball team in the United States.

If you see the team in Harlem, do not leave when the game is over. Many of the Rens, such as Clarence "Fats" Jenkins, Wee Willie Smith, Eyre "Bruiser" Saitch, and "Tarzan" Cooper, stay around to dance with the ladies when the postgame band strikes up a melody.

Harlem tourists may also get to see the Rens when they return to their homes in Cleveland, Chicago, Kansas City, and elsewhere. The team plays many games on the road. Because racism denies them the right to stay at hotels, however, they tour the country living in their specially equipped ten-thousand-dollar bus.

the "stompin' at the Savoy" never stops. When one band finishes the next begins without missing a beat.

Among the world-class musicians who entertain at the Savoy is Fletcher Henderson and his Rainbow Orchestra, who play until 12:30 A.M. at the all-white Roseland Ballroom in New York City, and then travels up to Harlem to play at the Savoy until 3:30 in the morning.

Another star of the Savoy is drummer Chick Webb. In addition to driving the beat like a railroad train running full throttle, Webb has hired some of the best musicians in the world for his band. These include trumpeter Cootie Williams and alto saxophonist Benny Carter.

People exit the Savoy after a night of dancing. The Savoy's vast ballroom welcomes all patrons, black and white, rich and poor.

A major feature at the Savoy is the "Battle of the Bands," where guest bands from New York, Chicago, and New Orleans are pitted against Chick Webb's orchestra. Even jazz greats like Louis Armstrong, Cab Calloway, King Oliver, and Fess Williams fear battling Webb, who is usually judged winner by the cheering crowd. Sometimes tensions run so high during these highly charged battles that fistfights break out between fans of different bands.

Dancing at the Savoy

Music is just part of the show at the Savoy, and some say the best entertainment is provided free by the dancers that strut and jump on the famous dance floor. This 50-by-250-foot burnished maple and mahogany floor is a wonder in itself and sees so much shoe leather it must be replaced every three years. No wonder the Savoy bills itself as "The Home of Happy Feet." And some of the dance fads that have swept across the nation, such as the Lindy Hop, the Suzy Q, and the Shim Sham Shimmy, were invented at the Savoy.

Tourists and other casual dancers should avoid trying out their new steps on Tuesday nights when the "400 Club" hoofs up a storm at the Savoy. This group features professionals such as George "Shorty" Snowden, who is credited for inventing the Lindy Hop, which features pinwheel spins and "breakaways" in which the female dance partner is thrown and twirled high in the air with wild abandon.

Tips for Travelers

You will surely be marked as a tourist if you pronounce the name of the dance palace as SA-voy. Those in the know call it the Sa-VOY, with the emphasis on the second syllable.

George "Shorty" Snowden and a few other talented hoofers stake out the northeast corner of the Savoy. This area is called the "Cat's Corner," and any dancers with two left feet who stumble into it are liable to receive a good swift kick in the shins from one of the dancing cats.

Thirsty dancers can find relief at the Savoy's soda fountain (unlike other Harlem clubs, no bootleg liquor is served here). For a nickel you can try tall mugs of ginger ale and root-de-toot root beer. Steaks are also served at the fountain for a reasonable price.

Women tourists will be glad to know that ladies are admitted free to the Savoy on Thursday nights, known as "Kitchen Mechanics' Night" for the slang term applied to cooks and maids. Saturday night is known among locals as "Square Night" because this is when the fumble-footed, "unhip," white downtowners show up to crowd onto the dance floor. And, while Sundays cost an extra quarter for admission, it is well worth the price for those visiting Harlem. This is considered the most glamorous night of the week, and international movie stars and royalty are likely to be in the crowd.

The Cotton Club

While the Savoy is open to all, the Cotton Club—the hottest spot in Harlem and a symbol of the Jazz Age—is notorious for its "whites only" admission policy. Owned by gangsters' the club at 644 Lenox caters to America's biggest stars of stage and screen. On any given night tourists on the sidewalk can watch singer and actor Jimmy Durante, dancer Fred Astaire, singer Ethel Merman, and composer Irving Berlin exit their limousines and hurry in the club's front door. These folks come uptown to see

The Savoy provides hot jazz music for its patrons, but watching dancers like these may be the best entertainment of all.

the greatest black entertainers in history, such as Cab Calloway, Duke Ellington, Ella Fitzgerald, Bill "Bojangles" Robinson, and Louis Armstrong.

Inside the Cotton Club the horseshoe-shaped room is filled with artificial palm trees, vines, and flowers, to give it a jungle atmosphere. Elegantly appointed tables ring the room on two levels and face the huge dance floor.

Louis Armstrong is a frequent jazz performer at the legendary Cotton Club.

The black waiters are a study in elegance. They serve food with a flourish and entertain those who pay thirty dollars for a bottle of champagne by loudly popping the corks and letting them fly across the room.

The menu features "soul food" dishes like fried chicken and barbecued spareribs and also exotic Chinese and Mexican dishes. While the food is exorbitantly expensive, it is secondary to the Broadway-like floor shows that can last up to two hours.

The entertainment starts with a few numbers by the fabulous Duke Ellington's Jungle Band. As the ten-piece band plays a jazzy rhythm, known as the "Jungle Sound," a line of fifteen dancing chorus girls high-kicks onto the stage. (According to club rules these dancers must be over five feet six inches, be under twenty-one, and have a "high-yaller"—or light-skinned—complexion. Cab Calloway sang two songs based on this chorus line policy: "She's Tall, She's Tan and She's Terrific" and "Cotton Colored Gal of Mine.")

The chorus line is followed by male dancers whose dance steps are described as high-stepping, gyrating, and snake dancing. Some are contortionists, such as Earl "Snakehips" Tucker, who can twist his body into a pretzel shape. As many as fifteen acts can follow, including the scantily clad Edith Wilson, who does slapstick comedy and sings risqué songs.

For all its fun and frivolity, impeccable behavior is expected at the Cotton Club.

Those who talk too loudly or act rowdily, especially during the shows, will be warned by waiters. If the behavior persists the offender will be ejected by burly bouncers. Since the club is owned by gangsters, a bounced patron has little recourse but to leave immediately.

The modest exterior of the Cotton Club. Inside, a two-hour floor show includes world-class jazz groups that entertain the club's exclusively white patrons.

Elaborately costumed dancers entertain the crowd at the Cotton Club.

Connie's Inn

Another club that caters to a mostly white audience is Connie's Inn, located at 165 131st Street at Seventh. Black visitors are allowed if they have enough money. While the average check per person at the Garden of Joy might be two to four dollars per person, a night at Connie's can cost up to fifteen dollars per customer. Perhaps this is why the club is filled with Harlem socialites. As a review in the *Daily News* says: "Should a blindfolded schoolboy poke a [straw] through the doorway of . . . Connie's Inn . . . on any night after midnight and take a random shot [with a bean], he would be almost sure to pop a Broadway playboy, a rich bootlegger, an actress or a society favorite on the chin."[31]

While the prices may be beyond your means, some tourists gather outside the wide red canopy that links the street to the club's door just to watch the high-society fashion show. If you are fortunate enough to gain entry to the club, you will walk downstairs to a room with a low ceiling where tables are very close together. According to the *Daily News:*

[A] man must trail the waiter to his seat with extreme caution lest he slide into some haughty young thing's lap [along the way]. Perhaps it wouldn't seem too cynical to remark here that . . . [the] owners of the Inn had more than this "illusion of intimacy" in mind when they laid the tables out. It may have been that they planned to squeeze in as many suckers as possible. But even so, the place will only hold about 125 couples.[32]

The tightly packed customers are seated around Connie's dance floor, which is itself surrounded by a miniature village about three feet high with scale models of bungalows, villas, and churches. Low-watt lights are set inside the little buildings and shine through the windows to evoke a sense of home. This stands in sharp contrast to the actual atmosphere of rude waiters and overpriced food and drink in this den of status-conscious social seekers. As the *Daily News* says: "If you are looking for real Harlem atmosphere, [Connie's] is one of the places not to go."[33]

Despite this, Connie's still hosts some of the best music in Harlem. Fats Waller started working here as a delivery

Racial Attitudes in Clubs

Sad to say, the divide between black and white does not stop at the dance hall door. While it is not uncommon to see a group of white patrons in a black Harlem club, black people are strictly forbidden from entering the Cotton Club. Although it is located in Harlem, the expensive, gangster-owned club—which is decorated in the style of a nineteenth-century southern mansion—caters only to whites. All waiters and waitresses are black, as are the dancers, singers, comedians, and other entertainers who appear alongside Duke Ellington and other world-class acts. The club's music, plantation theme, and raucous dance pieces allow wealthy white people a chance to experience what is called a primitive African or jungle atmosphere.

As a result of these white-only policies, tensions run high in African American establishments when white folks arrive. The following article by Randolph Edmonds from the *Messenger* newspaper, quoted in *The Cotton Club* by Jim Haskins, describes one such incident:

There was a public dance in the old Palace Casino one night. Two white fellows walked in the place and commenced dancing with some of the ladies of color, immediately there was a young riot. The ladies and gentlemen stormed the manager's office, and threatened all kinds of wild happenings if the white intruders were not ejected. The manager ordered the music stopped, and with a great show of race patriotism, ordered the two men to go downtown and dance with their white women and stop breaking up his business. I have seen this duplicated at the Renaissance [Casino] and other places in a lesser degree.

Connie's Inn, one of the more expensive clubs, features crowd-pleasing entertainers like dancer Bill "Bojangles" Robinson.

boy in 1920. Today he is the top performer and can be heard weekly at Connie's playing songs such as "Ain't Misbehavin'" and "What Did I Do to Be So Black and Blue," from his Broadway musical revue *Hot Chocolates*. Other performers at the Inn include Bill "Bojangles" Robinson and Earl "Snakehips" Tucker.

Where to Meet Jazz Musicians

True jazz aficionados can avoid the sky-high prices at Connie's and simply visit the several Harlem nightclubs that arc "hangouts" for the jazz musicians themselves. The Band Box Club on 161 131st Street is one such club. Run by cornet blower Addington Major, the back room attracts a steady stream of musicians who play all night at impromptu "jam" sessions. Drinks are of the fifty-cent variety, and there is certainly no doorman to keep out black, tan, red, white, or yellow. In fact the spirit of camaraderie found here between the musicians—many of whom served together in the Harlem Hellfighters—is in the true spirit of today's Harlem Renaissance.

Another hot spot for jam sessions is not a club at all but an open-air lot at 131st and Seventh. Known as "The Corner," this hangout attracts crowds of saxophonists, clarinetists, trumpet players, guitarists, and other musicians in all but the worst weather.

Across the street from this lot, in front of the Lafayette Theater, you can

Buy Records from "The Three Smiths"

Visitors to Harlem variety stores will be able to find phonograph records here that are usually unavailable elsewhere. Blues records in particular are found in large abundance, especially those of "The Three Smiths"—Bessie, Mamie, and Clara. Though not sisters these women personify the blues, that unique black folk music that is garnering nearly as much attention as jazz.

Clara Smith is called the "World's Greatest Moaner," for her ability to make her voice sound like a wailing saxophone or a crying clarinet. As Carl Van Vechten wrote in *Vanity Fair,* Smith's voice "tears the blood from one's heart."

Clara is second only to Bessie Smith, the legendary blues singer who became known as the "Empress of the Blues" after her Columbia record "Down-Hearted Blues" sold a record-setting 780,000 copies in six months. In Harlem, however, one of Bessie Smith's most beloved recordings, "Gimme a Pigfoot and a Bottle of Beer" is performed by many musicians.

Mamie Smith is known for "Crazy Blues," the first song ever recorded by a black soloist. Originally called "Harlem Blues", the name was changed by the record company to appeal to a white audience. After selling seventy-five thousand copies, Mamie Smith has recorded twenty-nine more records in the past several years. In addition to buying her records, tourists in Harlem might be able to catch her show, "Mamie Smith's Jazz Hounds."

She also livens the crowds with her high, clear voice in musical revues at the Lafayette and Lincoln theaters.

The vibrant Bessie Smith, known as the "Empress of the Blues."

also hear music played under the "Tree of Hope," a majestic elm with allegedly magical powers. No one knows how the myth got started, but it is believed that the Tree of Hope works like a kind of wishing well: Those who stroke, touch, or kiss the bark of the tree are said to have their wishes granted. Entertainers who wish upon the Tree of Hope believe that they will get a big break, their show will run a long time, or they will be hired in a better club. Tourists may see dancers practicing moves around the tree, or musicians playing music beneath its spreading branches.

The more hopeless crowd tends to gather at Kaiser's, located at 212 West 133rd Street. In this dark basement club, musicians meet to play music and smoke marijuana.

Leroy's at 2220 Fifth Avenue is another cellar club and one of Harlem's oldest cabarets. This place attracts black prizefighters, as well as musicians and other dandies and "swells" from Harlem nightlife.

The Gay Nightlife

Harlem is known to feature some wild entertainment, including "drag" balls where men dress as women in fine furs, bangles, high heels, and boas, while women dress as men with tuxedos, top hats, and canes. The Manhattan Casino/ Rockland Palace, at 280 West 155th Street, is famed for its monthly jazz drag balls that can attract up to six thousand people, many of them tourists and locals who come to gawk. The *Interstate Tattler* describes the scene, writing that a "costume ball can be a very tame thing. . . . But when all the exquisitely gowned women on the floor are men and a number of the smartest men are women, ah then, we have something over which to thrill and grow round-eyed."[34]

While the drag balls are monthly affairs, other clubs, such as the always-crowded Hollywood Cabaret at 41 West 125th Street, are known for featuring what is called "pansy entertainment." The One-Hundred-One Ranch Club on 101 West 139th Street, for example, has a "drag-queen" chorus line and is also the place where lines of patrons simultaneously perform the tap dance known as the Shim Sham Shimmy.

Capital of Jazz

Whether your taste in entertainment is flamboyant and gay or simple and unadorned, you will find music to suit your appetites in Harlem. For where else can a tourist listen to Duke Ellington at a glittering ballroom and then hear, on the way back to the hotel, an austere saxophone blowing the blues in an alley at midnight? If the Roaring Twenties are the Jazz Age, then surely Harlem can claim the title of the world capital of jazz. For the visitor, there could not be a better time to prick up your ears and let the music of the new age sweep you away.

Chapter 5

Theater in Harlem

The literary contributions of black authors and playwrights are well known. Black live theater stands unmatched in popularity and acceptance by black and white society alike in New York today.

African American theater in Harlem can trace its roots to around 1910, when black actors and actresses began forming their own theater companies to perform plays written by black authors for all-black audiences. Supported by the upper class on Sugar Hill and Strivers Row, African American acting companies were able to fill the seats in Harlem nearly every weekend.

While this atmosphere acted as a cauldron of creativity and talent, popular black shows such as *The Creole Show* and *Darktown Follies* were banned from New York's Broadway theater district.

However, these shows were the first to attract white audiences to Harlem, including the producer Florenz Ziegfeld, who adapted black song-and-dance numbers for his famed Ziegfeld Follies, seen by hundreds of thousands of white theatergoers.

Harlem's Great Theaters and Acting Companies

At no time in history have there been so many theater groups in Harlem. Tourists who wish to attend amateur theater may have a hard time choosing between the Dunbar Garden Players, the Harlem Experimental Theater, the Harlem Community Players, the Krigwa Players, the Negro Art Theatre, the Utopia Players, and others. Typical among these groups is the Ethiopian Players, which was founded in 1923 to perform classics such as Oscar Wilde's *Salomé* and Shakespeare's *Comedy of Errors*.

While most amateur theater groups produce plays that do not have black themes, they represent culturally elevated—and inexpensive—theatrical entertainment accessible to tourists on a budget. Check ads in local newspapers for theaters, times, and ticket prices.

Other Harlem acting companies have achieved great success in the past few years. The Harlem-based Provincetown Players, for example, gained national attention recently with a performance of Eugene O'Neill's *All God's Chillun Got Wings* at the Provincetown Playhouse, 133 MacDougal Street in Greenwich Village. In this play the great black actor Paul Robeson plays a boy who falls in love and marries a white girl played by the white actress Mary Blair. Since this represents the first time a black-white love story has ever been performed on a New York stage, *All God's Chillun Got Wings* has generated national controversy. Many newspaper editorials called for the play to be banned, and some implied there would be riots if the performance was allowed to take place. Naturally the controversy generated great interest and good box-office sales, and garnered international raves for Robeson.

Both the Lafayette (2235 Seventh Avenue) and the Lincoln (58 West 135th Street) theaters have excellent theater companies that have been able to translate their years of practice into success on Broadway. The Lafayette Players made their name performing well-received dramatic works such as *Madam X, The Love of Choo Chin,* and other plays.

The Harlem Renaissance Hits Broadway

Today Harlem tourists can take a bus, subway, or cab over to Broadway to see the work of some of the greatest African American singers, dancers, and playwrights in history. While blacks were initially banned from Broadway theaters, color began to seep into the Great White Way around 1920. The color of money, that is, as Broadway producers realized that white audiences would pay top dollar to see plays and musical revues featuring black performers.

The first play to break the Broadway color barrier was Eugene O'Neill's *The Emperor Jones,* which opened in November 1920. This play, which had premiered earlier that month with the Provincetown Players in Greenwich Village, was the first dramatic production in an all-white theater to star Charles Gilpin, an African American actor who became famous virtually overnight for his role in the play.

In 1924 the musical revue *Dixie to Broadway,* starring Florence Mills, featured an African American cast. The music was written by Will Vodery, an African American, who arranged music for the renowned Ziegfeld Follies for twenty-three years.

When Garland Anderson's *Appearances* opened at the Frolic Theatre on Broadway in October 1925, this was the first full-length Broadway play written by an African American.

A large crowd mingles during intermission at the Lafayette Theater. The reputation of Harlem's theater companies attracts many tourists.

The Lafayette holds fifteen hundred people and is the first New York City theater to integrate—that is, allow both black and white patrons. While plays are performed upstairs, the basement is home of the Hoofers' Club, where tap dancers such as Bill "Bojangles" Robinson, Honi Coles, Bunny Briggs, and Baby Laurence hold court nearly every night. In the informal atmosphere of the Hoofers' Club, tourists can have a drink with some of the most talented dancers of the jazz age. But do not bring your dancing shoes unless you can compete with the best.

The one-thousand-seat Lincoln, built in 1909, boasts a ten-thousand-dollar Wurlitzer organ. If you are lucky enough to be in Harlem at the right time, you might hear Fats Waller playing the organ for a silent movie. This booming organ is also played by other talented keyboardists during theater productions, jazz concerts, and vaudeville acts.

Other Harlem Theaters

While the Lincoln and Lafayette are Harlem's grand old theaters, they are by no means the only places to see music and plays in Harlem.

The Apollo Theater (253 West 125th Street) is quickly becoming a Harlem institution. In February of this year, the play *Harlem* began its run at the Apollo and, naturally, attracted great crowds from the local neighborhood. *Harlem* portrays "real life" in a railroad flat, with a black family from the South struggling to survive in the big city. Written by Wallace Thurman and featuring a cast of sixty black actors, the play is a must-see for Harlem tourists.

While the schedule changes regularly, it is worth a trip to the Harlem Opera House (207 West 125th Street), one of the most beautiful theaters in New York. Built in 1889, the eighteen-hundred-seat theater looks like a European palace on the outside and has a large gilded foyer inside. The opera house might show a play one night, a movie the next, and have an amateur contest hosted by Chick Webb's jazz orchestra on another night. The amateur contest gives singers, dancers, and other entertainers a chance to perform with one of Harlem's finest jazz bands. If you think you have the talent to try out, be aware: Audiences in Harlem can be very critical and will boo, yell, and even throw things at performers deemed to be unworthy.

Harlem Hits Broadway: Musical Revues

The first black productions that were widely seen by white audiences were musical revues, that is, shows that featured comedy skits, songs, and dances that satirized current events, trends, and celebrities.

The Harlem Renaissance came to Broadway in 1921 when Shuffle Along *opened to critical acclaim.*

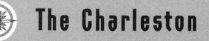

The Charleston

One of the plays that followed in the wake of *Shuffle Along* is *Runnin' Wild*, which opened at the Colonial Theater on upper Broadway a few years ago. This revue is well known for spawning the Charleston dance craze. This dance, which was known only to black people, was introduced to white America in the play, and has since become a craze around the world.

The music for the dance was written by New Jersey–born stride pianist James P. Johnson who wrote 230 songs, 19 symphonic works, and 11 musicals. But his most famous composition was "The Charleston," which has become synonymous with the Jazz Age.

The Charleston dance craze that began on Broadway has swept the world.

On May 23, 1921, the revue, *Shuffle Along*, written by Noble Sissle and Eubie Blake, put the Harlem Renaissance on-stage on Broadway for the first time. Filled with comedy, ragtime music, and jazz dancing, *Shuffle Along* was the first major production in many years to be produced, written, and performed entirely by African Americans. When the revue opened at the 63rd Street Music Hall above Times Square, white people flocked to it in droves, and police were forced to convert 63rd Street into a one-way thoroughfare to ease the traffic.

Within months records of songs from the revue, such as "I'm Just Wild About Harry" and "In Honeysuckle Time," became international best sellers. Actors and dancers from *Shuffle Along* also gained widespread recognition: Josephine

Baker, now an international star and the toast of the town in Paris, was an unknown dancer in the chorus line. Likewise Florence Mills became a star overnight when cast in the lead role. In the following weeks Mills adopted for a theme song "I'm a Little Blackbird Looking for a Bluebird," which was recognized as a thinly veiled protest against racism. When she met her unfortunate death from appendicitis in November 1927, Mills was planning to build a world-class black theater in Harlem.

Dance legend Bill "Bojangles" Robinson tap dances his way up a flight of stairs.

Shuffle Along ran on Broadway until 1925 and spawned dozens of imitators, such as *Put and Take* and *Strut Miss Lizzie*, which can be seen today still performed by acting companies in Harlem. There is also talk of reviving *Shuffle Along*. Tourists hoping to see this and other all-black productions should keep abreast of further developments through the *Amsterdam News* and other Harlem-based publications.

After the success of *Shuffle Along*, Sissle and Blake wrote other musicals including the *Chocolate Dandies* featuring Josephine Baker, which can be seen at the New Colonial Theater at 1887 Broadway at 62nd Street. Blake has also done solo projects such as the musical *Blackbirds*, featuring such talents as singers Mills and Ethel Waters and dance legend Bill "Bojangles" Robinson.

While the original *Blackbirds* can be seen today at the Alhambra (2110 Seventh Avenue) in Harlem, a revival of the revue *Blackbirds of 1928* is playing at the Liberty Theater at 234 West 42nd Street in the very heart of the Broadway theater district. The revue features Bill "Bojangles" Robinson, who tap dances his way up and down a set of stairs without missing a beat. After his first performance in the play, Robinson was labeled the greatest tap dancer in the world by theater critics.

In addition *Blackbirds of 1928* features songs such as "Diga Diga Doo" and "I Can't Give You Anything But Love" that have since become international hits. Harlem tourists will definitely want to make the trip to Broadway to see this play. As Johnson writes, the show has become a "New York institution; and out-of-town visitors [come] to the city with the conviction that it [is] something that [has] to be seen."[35] Of course, if you live in a large city such as Cleveland or Chicago, you might be able to see *Blackbirds of 1928* performed by the national touring company.

Other popular black revues playing on Broadway include *Rang Tang*, currently playing at the Majestic Theater, 247 West 44th Street, and *Keep Shufflin'*, playing at the Coburn Theatre, 22 West 63rd Street. Music for *Keep Shufflin'* was written by the incredible Fats Waller who also plays organ in the show. Meanwhile another Waller production, *1929 Hot Chocolates*, is being performed at the Hudson Theater, 141 West 44th Street. This show originated at Connie's Inn before landing on Broadway, and tourists can often see Waller performing various numbers from the productions at Connie's.

Serious Drama

The success of African American music revues has paved the way for dramatic plays with black casts. These shows, mostly written by white playwrights, attempt to accurately depict black life. In 1927 Paul Green's *In Abraham's Bosom*

opened at the Provincetown Playhouse. This play, which won a Pulitzer Prize in 1927, portrays a black farmer who struggles against society to obtain an education. In the end he kills his white half-brother and is hanged by a mob.

When the drama *Porgy*, written by DuBose and Dorothy Heyward, premiered on October 1, 1927 at the Guild Theater, 245 West 52nd Street, it was a high point for Harlem theater. The play, which can still be seen today at the Guild, features a who's who of Harlem actors. The ticket prices are high, as much as twenty-five dollars, and the Guild is a segregated theater. So while many Harlem actors are in the cast, only the richest folk on Strivers Row can afford a ticket—and then they are forced to sit in the colored section in the balcony.

In February 1928 *Meek Mose* opened at the Princess Theater at 104 West 39th Street. The play was written by Frank Wilson, who also plays the title role in *Porgy*. On opening night hearts in Harlem swelled with pride when New York mayor Jimmy Walker attended with many members of the city's upper classes.

Finally, tourists visiting Broadway via Harlem should try to make time to see *The Green Pastures* at the Mansfield Theater, 246 West 47th Street. This play by Marc Connelly focuses on African American tales of spirituality using various Bible stories and figures, or—as the playwright describes it—is "an attempt to present certain aspects of a living religion in the terms of its believers. The religion is that of thousands of Negroes in the deep South."[36]

If you need any more inspiration to see the play, read Johnson's praise for *The Green Pastures*:

[In previous dramas the] Negro removed any lingering doubts as to his ability to do intelligent acting. In *The Green Pastures* he established conclusively his capacity to get the utmost subtleties cross the footlights, to convey the most delicate nuances of emotion, to create the atmosphere in which the seemingly unreal becomes for the audience the most real thing in life. *The Green Pastures* is a play so simple and yet so profound, so close to the earth and yet so spiritual, that it is as high a test for those powers in the actor as

Multitalented jazz pianist Fats Waller wrote several of the black revues now playing on Broadway, including the hugely popular Keep Shufflin'.

any play the American stage has seen—a higher test than many of the immortalized classics. . . . The acting in *The Green Pastures* seems so spontaneous and natural that one is tempted to believe the players are not really acting. In the light of the truth about the matter, this is a high compliment. . . . What Mr. Connelly actually did was to work something very little short of a miracle. No one seems able to remember any playwright, play, and company of players that have together received such unanimous praise as these three factors in the making of *The Green Pastures.*[37]

Creator of Laughter, Songs, and Dances

Only twenty-five years ago African Americans were relegated to playing buffoons,

criminals, butlers, or maids in theatrical productions. Today, as Johnson writes: "Beginning as a mere butt of laughter [the black actor] has worked on up through [minstrel] and musical-comedy shows to become the creator of laughter; to become a maker of songs and dances for people."[38]

This has created a great situation for the Harlem tourist, with nearly a dozen black plays and revues playing on any given night in Harlem and on Broadway, the theater capital of the world. So do yourself a favor, save up a few extra dollars, and put the theater on your travel schedule when you visit Harlem, the neighborhood with more black talent per square block than any other place in the world.

Chapter 6

The Arts in Harlem

Tourists visiting Harlem would be wrong to assume that the Harlem Renaissance revolves exclusively around attending musical revues, listening to jazz, and dancing in speakeasies. In fact some of the literary leaders of the New Negro Movement have come to disdain the rowdy drunken behavior that passes for a renaissance in their neighborhood. It was, after all, the writers and painters who first attracted national interest in Harlem and its people.

The catalyst for this movement can be traced to a dinner held, not in Harlem, but on Fifth Avenue at the Civic Club near Twelfth Street. The Civic Club is one of the few high-society establishments in New York City that has no gender or racial barriers. On March 21, 1924, Uptown joined Downtown when white publishers, editors, and writers from some of New York's biggest publishing houses and magazines met with young authors, intellectuals, poets, and illustrators of the New Negro Movement.

Alain Locke was the master of ceremonies, and at least 110 people were in attendance. Hopes were high for this meeting where authors and publishers made optimistic speeches about the movement. As editor of *Century* magazine, Carl Van Doren, stated: "What American literature decidedly needs at this moment is color, music, gusto, the free expression of [happy] or desperate moods. If the Negroes are not in a position to contribute these items, I do not know what Americans are."[39]

The meeting bore fruit in the following months. *Harper's* magazine published the poetry of Countee Cullen; Alfred Knopf was inspired to publish Langston Hughes's first book, *The Weary Blues*; the Black Writers' Guild was formed; and

75

the *Survey Graphic* dedicated several full issues to contemporary black life. These issues were later compiled into Locke's *The New Negro: An Interpretation*, which is credited for presenting the politics, poetry, and literary talents of the renaissance to a national audience.

While tourists to Harlem may be more familiar with Duke Ellington, Bessie Smith, Josephine Baker, and Paul Robeson, the center of intellectual life in Harlem revolves around Langston Hughes, Alain Locke, W.E.B. Du Bois, Countee Cullen, and other writers. And for the traveler who is interested in scholarly pursuits, Harlem is at the forefront of modern African American insight.

The Public Library

The Harlem branch of the New York Public Library at 103 West 135th Street is the center of intellectual and cultural activity in Harlem, and a visit to this magnificent building should be on every tourist's agenda. The library is staffed by college-educated black women whose influence is reflected in the large, permanent collection of books about black culture.

In 1926 this already wonderful collection was enhanced when the Carnegie Corporation purchased Arthur Schomburg's collection for the New York Public Library. Schomburg, a black Puerto Rican born in 1874, had a thirst for knowledge about people of African descent and spent his life collecting

Harlem is home to many talented writers and intellectuals, such as poet Countee Cullen (pictured).

books, letters, manuscripts, prints, playbills, paintings, and artifacts by and about black people.

Since its purchase Schomburg's collection has become the cornerstone of the New York Public Library's Division of Negro Literature, History, and Prints. Many of the ten thousand items in the collection are frequently on loan to the 135th Street branch and can be seen in the reading room. In addition to black art and literature dating back centuries, visitors to the Harlem branch might see Schomburg talking to patrons or conducting seminars with scholars and writers of the New Negro Movement.

Access to the works of great black authors and artists may also be as close as your corner newsstand, where their brash, sometimes revolutionary, work can be found in newspapers such as the *Messenger, Challenge,* the *Voice,* the *Crusader,* and the *Emancipator.* These papers, which can also be found in restaurants, candy stores, and barbershops, give a unique glimpse into the minds of young black talent in Harlem today. They also provide valuable tips and insights into the neighborhood that can be of use to travelers and locals alike.

The Dark Tower Events

The library and The Hobby Horse are the best places for you to meet the literary elite in Harlem. While the average tourist might be limited to these venues, if you are able to befriend one of the young talents—or if you are an aspiring author or artist reading this guide—the hottest ticket in town is an invitation to the salon, or literary gathering, at the home of A'Lelia Walker.

Walker is the daughter of the famous Madame C.J. Walker, a poor orphan who grew up and made millions in the 1910s selling "Madame Walker's Wonderful Hair Grower" and "hot combs" to straighten the hair of black women. When Madame Walker died in 1919, A'Lelia inherited her mother's spectacular townhouses at 108–110 West 136th Street.

Walker is probably the most flamboyant character of the Harlem Renaissance and is called the "joy-goddess"[40] of Harlem by Langston Hughes. Standing six foot three inches in her high heels, the heiress to the hair-straightening fortune dresses in brightly colored silks, ermine, and sable, with silver turbans, glittering diamonds, and gleaming ropes of pearls.

In 1928 Walker began holding the salon in her mansion. She named the literary gathering the Dark Tower after Countee Cullen's popular column in *Opportunity* magazine. Walker's Dark Tower gatherings feature music, art, and poetry readings by members of Harlem's creative community.

If you are fortunate enough to obtain an invitation to the Dark Tower, you can expect to enter the townhouses through two tall French doors. Follow the blue velvet rug down the long hallway to Walker's beautifully appointed tearoom. Upstairs, in the library on the top floor of the townhouse, intellectual conversations and games of bridge take place amid heavy wooden bookcases filled with books by black authors. Downstairs, on the main floor, salon patrons drink the finest wines and liqueurs and marvel at Walker's talking parrot. Entertainment

Tips for Travelers

If you are interested in meeting some of Harlem's hot new authors, they often meet at The Hobby Horse bookstore, 205 West 136th Street.

often consists of the hottest black stars on Broadway and the Harlem cabaret circuit, including Alberta Hunter, the Four Bon Bons, and Jimmy Daniels.

Walker's money—and sense of humor—have allowed her to turn the racial customs of the outside world upside down. If you are a white guest, expect to be served food such as pig's feet, chitterlings, and bathtub gin—provisions common among working-class folks living in Harlem's railroad flats. Black visitors can expect to be served caviar, pheasant under glass, and pricey French champagne in the fanciest private rooms segregated from the white guests.

While the company may be sublime, the decorations in the townhouse are spectacular. Madame Walker's fortune has been used here to obtain the most expensive furniture, carpets, and serving sets in the world. Even the most sophisticated visitor cannot help but gape when they see Walker's sixty-thousand-

Millionaire A'Lelia Walker sits for a manicure. Her exclusive Dark Tower gatherings are the hottest ticket in town for members of Harlem's creative community.

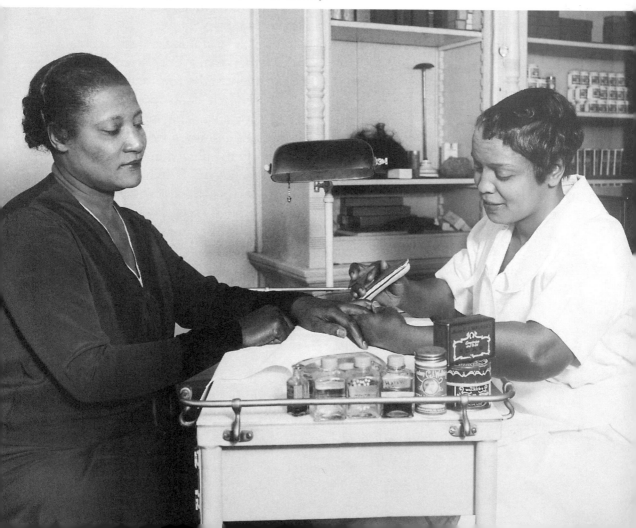

dollar pipe organ or her twenty-four-carat gold-plated piano.

Walker is also famous for her wild parties, which might be easier for you to cadge invitations to. Among the black-and-tan guests expect to find authors, artists, actors, and musicians along with an impressive array of Wall Street businessmen, socialites, royalty, rumrunning gangsters, club owners, and other Harlem regulars. Guests are greeted by black servants dressed in the style of the seventeenth century with white wigs, decorated jackets, and black stockings. These parties are often later reviewed in articles on the society pages of Harlem newspapers. One such review by Geraldyn Dismond in the *Interstate Tattler* may help prepare you if you attend such an event:

What a crowd! All classes and colors met face to face, ultra aristocrats, [middle classes], Communists, [wealthy] Park Avenuers galore, bookers, publishers, Broadway celebs, and Harlemites giving each other the once over. The social revolution was on. And yes, [shipping heiress] Lady Nancy Cunard was there all in black (she would) with 12 of her grand bracelets. . . . And was the entertainment on the up and up! Into swell dance music was injected African drums that played havoc with blood pressure. Jimmy Daniels sang his gigolo hits. Gus Simons, the Harlem crooner, [sang] the "River Stay Away From [My] Door" and

An Invitation to the Dark Tower

Entrance to A'Lelia Walker's Dark Tower salon is by invitation only. But as you can see from the following invitation, printed in *The Harlem Renaissance* by Steven Watson, you might be able to attend one of these stellar literary gatherings as a guest of an invited member:

We dedicate this tower to the aesthetes [those who cultivate an unusually high sensitivity to beauty in art]. That cultured group of young Negro writers, sculptors, painters, music artists, composers and their friends. A quiet place of particular charm. A rendezvous where they may feel at home to partake of a little tidbit amid pleasant, interesting atmosphere. Members only and those whom they wish to bring will be accepted. If you choose to become one of us you may register when first attending "The Dark Tower." One dollar a year. Open nine at eve 'til two in the morn.

Taylor [Gordon] brought out [shouts of] everything from "Hot Dog" to "Bravo" when he made high C.[41]

The Literary Gatherings of Jessie Fauset

Tourists can sometimes wrangle invitations to Walker's parties if they know the right people. Visitors with only the purest of literary intentions, however, can gain admission to the social gatherings of the influential novelist Jessie

Fauset. If you happen to be a visiting writer, poet, or playwright, Langston Hughes explains what you might expect to find at Fauset's 142nd Street apartment:

At . . . Fauset's parties there [is] always quite a different atmosphere from that at most other Harlem good-time gatherings. At Miss Fauset's, a good time [is] shared by talking literature and reading poetry aloud and perhaps enjoying some conversation in French. White people [are] seldom present there unless they [are] very distinguished white people because Jessie Fauset did not feel like opening her home to mere sightseers, or faddists momentarily in love with Negro life. At her house one . . . usually [meets] editors and students, writers and social workers, and serious people who [like] books and the British Museum, and had perhaps been to Florence. (Italy, not Alabama.)

I remember, one night at her home there was a gathering in

At Jessie Fauset's literary gatherings, her distinguished guests engage in spirited discussions of art and literature.

honor of Salvador de Madariaga, the Spanish diplomat . . . which somehow became a rather self-conscious gathering, with all the Harlem writers called upon to recite their poems and speak their pieces.[42]

Harlem Arts

Some of Harlem's greatest artists are seen at Fauset's and Walker's parties. In the past decade or so these painters, sculptors, printmakers, and photographers have come to portray realistic images of African American people and culture. These images stand in sharp contrast to the negative, racist images most often produced in the mainstream American press.

If you are visiting Harlem you owe it to yourself to seek out the works of these talented artists in galleries, museums, and elsewhere. One place to start is the Harlem branch of the New York Public Library where the works of great black artists are often on display. And the price is certainly right—admission to the library is free.

Have Your Picture Taken by the Best

Perhaps the most well-known and widely circulated images of present-day Harlem are photographs taken by James Van Der Zee. These pictures, such as his famous "Couple Wearing Raccoon

Poet, playwright, and novelist Langston Hughes is one of Harlem's leading literary figures.

Sculptor Meta Warrick Fuller's stunning bronze statue Ethiopia Awakening *is considered the starting point of the Harlem art renaissance.*

dings, barbershop customers, and pool-hall toughs. Some of the celebrities seen in his pictures include heavyweight champion Jack Johnson, dancer Bill "Bojangles" Robinson, and singers Florence Mills and Mamie Smith.

If you can pay the price, you can buy prints of Van Der Zee's work, or have your portrait taken by this world-class photographer simply by dropping into his studio, Guarantee Photo, on 135th Street.

Women Who Sculpt

Just as Van Der Zee's photos have come to be icons of the Harlem Renaissance, so too have the sculptures of Meta Warrick Fuller. Fuller, born in 1877, is one of the few academically trained African American artists of the New Negro Movement, having attended Pennsylvania Academy of Fine Arts in Philadelphia as well as the L'École des Beaux Arts in Paris.

As a black woman Fuller faced discrimination because of her gender as well as her race. In spite of this hardship, she creates her works in expressive and emotional celebrations of the black physique and African and African American culture. Her bronze statue, *Ethiopia Awakening,* sculpted in 1921, is considered the starting point of the Harlem art renaissance. The sculpture

Coats" posed with their expensive automobile, show a picture of black upper-class life rarely seen in the United States. Van Der Zee also photographs sports teams, family gatherings, funerals, wed-

portrays a noble African woman with the headdress of an Egyptian queen, her feet and legs wrapped like a mummy. Fuller's works may be seen at the "Making of America" exhibition at the Harlem Public Library.

Another woman who works wondrous art from clay and metal is Augusta Savage. Born in Florida, Savage had to fight racism to gain an art education af-

ter she was rejected for a summer art program in 1923 by the French government because of her race.

Despite this setback Savage became a portrait sculptor who portrayed many famous African Americans. In 1923 the New York Public Library commissioned Savage to create a bust of W.E.B. Du Bois, which can be seen displayed at the library. The work was highly regarded,

Portrait sculptor Augusta Savage examines two of her creations. Although Savage is one of Harlem's most celebrated artists, she often neglects her own work to nurture the talent of gifted children.

and Savage went on to portray Marcus Garvey, Frederick Douglass, James Weldon Johnson, and other black leaders.

Although she has garnered critical attention lately, Savage chooses to spend most of her time teaching young people the art of sculpture. Tourists in Harlem can meet the artist by visiting her studio in a storefront on 142nd Street and Seventh. Do not be afraid to stop in, but beware. The great artist may thrust a broom into your hands and order you to sweep up the studio, since she believes you must learn to clean up before you make a mess.

Harlem Painters

Painters are also a notable part of Harlem's art renaissance. Leading the way is Archibald J. Motley Jr., who is one of the first black artists to create work that focuses solely on African American life. Ironically, while Motley's paintings are strongly identified with the Harlem Renaissance, he works mainly in Chicago and Paris. Nonetheless Motley's famous *Blues,* which portrays a crowded room full of black people dancing to a blues band, is a scene that could be observed in Harlem cabarets any night of the week. Critics say the painting, in the style of cubism, gives form and color to the music and dance of the Harlem Renaissance.

Motley won a Gold Medal from the prestigious Harmon Foundation in 1926, and his work can be seen at various exhibitions throughout New York. Check local papers for listings.

Aaron Douglas is another midwesterner whose work has come to symbolize the Harlem Renaissance. Born in Topeka, Kansas, in 1899, Douglas has been living in Harlem since 1925. His work consists of angular, stylized figures presented in silhouette. Douglas often pre-

Harmon Foundation Exhibits

Harlem visitors interested in art should look for exhibits by the Harmon Foundation. This prestigious organization, named for white arts patron William E. Harmon, started awarding prizes for achievement in art in 1926, giving its first literary prize and four hundred dollars to Countee Cullen for his first volume of poetry, *Color.* Artist Palmer Hayden, who worked as a custodian to pay for art supplies, won the art prize.

Harmon Foundation exhibitions can be seen all over New York City—from Harlem, to Greenwich Village, to Downtown. Consult your local papers for galleries, addresses, and times. These art shows provide African American artists widespread exposure to the general public that they probably would not have otherwise. And the foundation has attracted black artists from all over. Within the last few years the number of artists in the Harmon Foundation registry has grown from about ten in 1926 to more than three hundred.

sents these characters in murals that incorporate themes such as biblical scenes, historical events, and farmers working in a field.

Revolutionary Artists

If you want to see Douglas's work, one of his beautiful murals can be viewed at the Club Harlem African Room, 388 Lenox. His paintings *Study for God's Trombones* and *Noah's Ark* are on display at the Harlem branch of the New York Public Library. Or simply pick up a copy of Wallace Thurman's new novel, *The Blacker the Berry;* Douglas illustrated the jacket cover. In addition the painter's work can be seen on illustrations and cover designs for many black publications, including the *Crisis* and *Opportunity.*

Douglas is currently working on a mural at Fisk University in Nashville, Tennessee, and has been commissioned to create one entitled *The Evolution of Negro Dance* for the new Harlem YMCA, which is currently in the planning stages.

Douglas, Fuller, and others are only a small sampling of revolutionary artists whose work today will influence generations to come. Just as visitors can hear jazz on almost every Harlem corner, so too can they view works by artists both amateur and famous. There has never been a better time to visit Harlem. And the streets of the neighborhood beckon to those who wish to find enrichment through music, dance, art, theater, and literature.

Notes

Introduction: A New Day in Harlem
1. Alain Locke, ed., *The New Negro: An Interpretation*. New York: Arno, 1968, p. 3.
2. Quoted in Locke, *The New Negro*, p. 301.

Chapter One: The World's Greatest Negro Metropolis
3. Quoted in Locke, *The New Negro*, p. 305.
4. Quoted in Locke, *The New Negro*, p. 308.
5. Locke, *The New Negro*, p. 6
6. "Old Fifteenth Given Rousing Reception," *New York Age*, February 22, 1919.
7. Quoted in Locke, *The New Negro*, pp. 302–3.

Chapter Two: Harlem Basics
8. James Weldon Johnson, *Black Manhattan*. New York: Arno and the *New York Times*, 1968, p. 160.
9. Quoted in Nathan Irvin Huggins, ed., *Voices from the Harlem Renaissance*. New York: Oxford University Press, 1976, p. 90.
10. Quoted in Huggins, *Voices from the Harlem Renaissance*, pp. 110–11.
11. Quoted in Jervis Anderson, *This Was Harlem*. New York: Farrar Straus Giroux, 1982, p. 341.
12. Quoted in Steven Watson, *The Harlem Renaissance*. New York: Pantheon, 1995, p. 89.
13. Quoted in Watson, *The Harlem Renaissance*, p. 5.
14. Allon Schoener, ed., *Harlem on My Mind*. New York: Random House, 1995, p. 80.
15. Johnson, *Black Manhattan*, pp. 162–63.
16. Rudolph Fisher, *The Walls of Jericho*. New York: Alfred A. Knopf, 1928, p. 189.
17. Johnson, *Black Manhattan*, p. 163.
18. Quoted in Anderson, *This Was Harlem*, p. 248.
19. Quoted in Watson, *The Harlem Renaissance*, p. 80.

Chapter Three: Eating and Drinking and Gambling in Harlem
20. Jimmy Durante and Jack Kofold, *Night Clubs*. New York: Alfred A. Knopf, 1930, p. 113.
21. Quoted in Huggins, *Voices from the Harlem Renaissance*, p. 46.
22. Quoted in Huggins, *Voices from the Harlem Renaissance*, p. 118.
23. Quoted in Huggins, *Voices from the Harlem Renaissance*, p. 371.

24. Quoted in Huggins, *Voices from the Harlem Renaissance*, p. 74.
25. Wallace Thurman, *Negro Life in New York's Harlem*. Girard, KS: Haldeman-Julius, 1928, p. 30.
26. Quoted in Schoener, *Harlem on My Mind*, p. 85.
27. Quoted in Schoener, *Harlem on My Mind*, p. 80.

Chapter Four: Jazz and Dance in Harlem

28. Johnson, *Black Manhattan*, pp. 160–61.
29. Schoener, *Harlem on My Mind*, p. 80.
30. Quoted in Huggins, *Voices from the Harlem Renaissance*, p. 77.
31. Quoted in Schoener, *Harlem on My Mind*, pp. 82–83.
32. Quoted in Schoener, *Harlem on My Mind*, p. 83.
33. Quoted in Schoener, *Harlem on My Mind*, p. 83.
34. Quoted in Watson, *The Harlem Renaissance*, p. 136.

Chapter Five: Theater in Harlem

35. Johnson, *Black Manhattan*, p. 212.
36. Quoted in Johnson, *Black Manhattan*, p. 219.
37. Johnson, *Black Manhattan*, pp. 218–19.
38. Johnson, *Black Manhattan*, p. 224.

Chapter Six: The Arts in Harlem

39. Quoted in Watson, *The Harlem Renaissance*, p. 28.
40. Quoted in Huggins, *Voices from the Harlem Renaissance*, p. 96.
41. Quoted in Huggins, *Voices from the Harlem Renaissance*, p 95.
42. Quoted in Huggins, *Voices from the Harlem Renaissance*, p. 97.

For Further Reading

Books

Ann Graham Gaines, *The Harlem Renaissance in American History*. Berkeley Heights, NJ: Enslow, 2002. The rebirth of black literature, music, and art that took place in New York in the 1920s.

P. Stephen Hardy and Sheila Jackson Hardy, *Extraordinary People of the Harlem Renaissance*. New York: Childrens, 2000. Looks at the many artists, photographers, choreographers, musicians, composers, poets, writers, and other creative people whose work was the basis for the Harlem Renaissance.

Stuart A. Kallen, ed., *The Roaring Twenties*. San Diego: Greenhaven, 2002. Narratives and eyewitness accounts of the 1920s with essays on politics, fashion, music, movies, and daily life.

Martha E. Rhynes, *I, Too, Sing America: The Story of Langston Hughes*. Greensboro, NC: Morgan Reynolds, 2002. A biography of a man who became famous during the Harlem Renaissance for writing poems, stories, and books that celebrated African American heritage.

Steven Watson, *The Harlem Renaissance*. New York: Pantheon, 1995. A well-written, illustrated history exploring the hub of black culture in New York between 1920 and 1930.

Internet Sources

African American History, "Rhapsodies in Black," 1997. http://afroamhistory.about.com. A Web page with pictures of work by famous artists of the Harlem Renaissance with links to biographies and commentary on various aspects of the time.

Works Consulted

Books

Jervis Anderson, *This Was Harlem*. New York: Farrar Straus Giroux, 1982. A cultural portrait of Harlem between 1900 and 1950 with chapters on society, entertainment, and prominent members of the Harlem Renaissance.

Jimmy Durante and Jack Kofold, *Night Clubs*. New York: Alfred A. Knopf, 1930. A short book about New York nightspots written by Durante, the renowned singer, dancer, and comedian who was a habitué of Harlem during the renaissance.

Rudolph Fisher, *The Walls of Jericho*. New York: Alfred A. Knopf, 1928. A fictional account of a man who buys a house on the border between the white and black sections of Harlem in the 1920s. The novel details the difficulties faced by educated African Americans who tried to blend into white society.

Jim Haskins, *The Cotton Club*. New York: Random House, 1977. The illustrated history of Harlem's hottest nightclub where stars of stage and screen dined and danced to the sounds of the greatest jazz bands in history.

Nathan Irvin Huggins, ed., *Voices from the Harlem Renaissance*. New York: Oxford University Press, 1976. Articles about black politics, culture, art, and religion from well-known writers of the Harlem Renaissance, including Marcus Garvey, Countee Cullen, Nancy Cunard, W.E.B. Du Bois, Langston Hughes, and others.

James Weldon Johnson, *Black Manhattan*. New York: Arno and the *New York Times,* 1968. A history of black culture in New York City from the seventeenth century to 1930, when this book by the renowned literary talent of the Harlem Renaissance was first published.

Alain Locke, ed., *The New Negro: An Interpretation*. New York: Arno, 1968. First published in 1925, this book—with its series of articles, essays, poems, and stories by black authors—brought worldwide attention to the literary movement of the Harlem Renaissance.

Allon Schoener, ed., *Harlem on My Mind*. New York: Random House, 1995. An illustrated collection of newspaper articles from the *New York Times*, the *Negro World, Amsterdam News*, and dozens of other papers concerning events in Harlem between 1900 and 1968.

Wallace Thurman, *Negro Life in New York's Harlem*. Girard, KS: Haldeman-Julius, 1928. A poetic account of Harlem written during the height of the renaissance.

Periodicals

"Old Fifteenth Given Rousing Reception," *New York Age*, February 22, 1919. An article about the march through Harlem of the all-black 369th Infantry Regiment, formerly known as the Fifteenth Regiment of New York's National Guard.

Internet Sources

American Social History Project, "The 'New Negro,'" 2001. www.ashp.cuny.edu/video/up6.html. A website guide to the documentary series *Who Built America*, about black contributions to American society.

Index

Picture Credits

About the Author

Stuart A. Kallen is the author of more than 150 nonfiction books for children and young adults. He has written on topics ranging from the theory of relativity to the history of rock and roll. In addition, Mr. Kallen has written award-winning children's videos and television scripts. In his spare time, Stuart A. Kallen is a singer/songwriter/guitarist in San Diego, California.